MIND OVER HEAD CHATTER:

THE PSYCHOLOGY OF

ATHLETIC SUCCESS

Volume II

ART STILL & GREG JUSTICE

ISBN-13: 978-0692951392 (Greg Justice)
ISBN-10: 0692951393

Cover design: Doug Coonrod

Book layout design & eBook conversion by manuscript2ebook.com

DEDICATION

If you have ever dreamed of being a champion,
this book is for you.

TABLE OF CONTENTS

Section III: Getting Centered

Section IV: We Are the Champions

ACKNOWLEDGMENTS

Greg Justice

First of all, I would like to thank my co-author, Art Still for sharing his story about going "from the projects to the pros" throughout this book.

This book is the result of playing, training, and coaching athletics at every level. My passion for sports and the study of successful athletes began when I was a child, playing little league baseball. It continued through high school and college as a wrestler and judo practitioner.

Upon completing my undergraduate and master's degrees, I managed a fitness center, where I met and trained Art and a few of his teammates from the Kansas City Chiefs.

Throughout my career, I have been blessed to work with football, basketball & baseball players, along with golfers, and wrestlers from grade school to world-class athletes. I would like to thank each of them for the lessons they taught me.

I would also like to thank my parents and coaches, as they helped make me the man I am today.

Thanks to my business partner at Scriptor Publishing Group, Kelli Watson for her help on this book. I would also like to thank Doug Coonrod, Heith Carnahan, David Justice and Pankaj Runthals for the design, layout, and editing of *Mind Over Head Chatter.*"

And, last but not least, a special thank you to my wife, Dana, who has supported all of my efforts from the very beginning. I couldn't have done it without you!

Art Still

For starters, during my 62 years here on earth I've been beyond fortunate to have come across individuals of all ages who have had a positive influence on the person I am today.

I didn't become the man I am today without the support of my parents. They instilled in me the values of treating others the way I would want to be treated and to be REPSECTFUL, RESPONSIBLE and ACCOUNTABLE for all of my actions. These values followed me throughout my youth, college and professional career as an athlete and person.

A special thanks goes to thank Greg Justice, my co-author and friend for opening up the opportunity for me to share more fully my passion with others, that of maintaining a healthy lifestyle whether an athlete or not. I met Greg in the early 80's at a health club he was managing. Greg's enthusiasm and passion for people is contagious. I'm thankful we reconnected and am working together to better the health and lives of individuals and families.

I also want to thank my neighbors that I was privileged to be with in Camden, New Jersey along with my classmates, teammates and teachers from Camden High School, especially my principal, Mrs. Cream and football coach, Andy Hinson and basketball coach, Clarence Turner. They helped and encouraged me to go to the next level.

I want to thank everyone, on and off the field at the University of Kentucky, especially my coaches, Fran Curci and Pat Etchenberry, where being RESPECTFUL, being RESPONSIBLE and being ACCOUNTABLE FOR MY ACTIONS was taken to another level.

Playing 12 years in the NFL left a lasting impression on my life, and I want to thank Marv Levy and Walt Corey for helping me become a better player and help shape the man I am today.

Finally, I would like to thank Scriptor Publishing for all of their hard work and help in getting *Mind Over Head Chatter* published and encouraging me on this adventure.

FOREWORD

Athletes of all ages are always looking for an edge. Youth, high school, college and pro athletes... heck, even aging fitness enthusiasts are always looking for peak performance.

In this extraordinary book on success and athletic performance, Greg Justice and Art Still reveal the methods and stories from some of the top athletes of all-time that includes topics like... belief, attitude, leadership, goal-setting, visualization, breath-work, and positive self-talk of champion athletes.

This is a MUST-read book if you are a coach, athlete, or parent of an athlete.

Todd Durkin, MA, CSCS
Owner, Fitness Quest 10
Lead Training Advisor, Under Armour
Author, The IMPACT! Body Plan

———~~~———

INTRODUCTION

Author's Note: *The introduction is a tribute to my friend and mentor, Fred Hatfield (aka: Dr. Squat). This is his book review of Mind Over Head Chatter Volume 1. He summed up the book so eloquently that I wanted to share it with the readers of this book.*

———✦———

Right out of the blocks, I said to myself, "This is going to be good!" You see, Justice begins his book with an excellent treatise on the criticality of passion in sports success. Had he begun his book any other way, it would have been just another how-to book on sports psychology. But he planted his feet in the concrete of what sports are all about, and made his stand. I was compelled to read further, and stayed up late finishing the book. Let me mention a few notable topics.

Sports are a team effort. You've all heard the slogans: "There is no I in Team." "Machine." "Division of labor." Stuff like that. Point is, regardless of what sport you're engaged in, you will need the support of all of your teammates, your coaches, your friends and family, even your doctor, physiotherapist, sports psychologist and nutritionist, for all are part of the team, and all share a common goal. Justice summarizes the research on the effects of team cohesion, and concludes that the "secret weapon" for all athletes is this sort of broad-based support. Each part of this base can be thought of as a spoke in the wheel.

The more spokes, the stronger the wheel. These are the "technologies" of sports training.

Back to passion, as it seems that in order to be a champion, this is the one common thread spoken of by athletes and coaches alike. Justice quotes many. Here are a few:

"Never let the fear of striking out get in your way. I swing big, with everything I've got. I hit big or I miss big. I like to live as big as I can."
— *Babe Ruth*

"To be a champion, you have to learn to handle stress and pressure. But if you've prepared mentally and physically, you don't have to worry."
— *Harvey McKay*

"There's always the motivation of wanting to win. Everybody has that. But a champion needs, in his attitude, a motivation above and beyond winning."
— *Pat Riley*

"Which player is mentally stronger? Which player is going to fight the hardest in the big points? These are the things that determine who is the champion."
— *Novak Djokovic*

"I hated every minute of training, but I said, 'Don't quit. Suffer now and live the rest of your life as a champion.'"
— *Muhammad Ali*

"The last three or four reps is what makes the muscle grow. This area of pain divides the champion from someone else who is not a champion. That's what most people lack, having the guts to go on and just say they'll go through the pain no matter what happens."
— *Arnold Schwarzenegger*

The ability to play under pressure, teachability and attitude all hinge on passion. Justice points out that it isn't just intrinsic elements such as DNA that go into creating a champion, it's also these and other extrinsic elements. In fact, all of Chapter Three can be summed up in this little affirmation:

PASSION IS...

NOT commitment to excellence...

> *Rather, utter disdain for anything less!*

NOT endless hours of practice...

> *Instead, PERFECT practice!*

NOT ability to cope...

> *Rather, total domination of EVERY situation in life!*

NOT setting goals...

> *Goals too often prescribe performance limits!*

NOT doing what it takes to win...

> *Instead, a burning commitment to do what no one has ever done -- or will ever do again!!*

NOT need to achieve...

> *Instead, doing what it takes to EXCEED the bounds of mere convention*

NOT force of skill or muscle...

> *Rather, it's the irrepressible, sometimes explosive, force of WILL!*

If you believe in and practice these things, then for you, winning is neither everything nor the only thing as the great Vince Lombardi once said. If you believe in and practice these things, then, for you, winning has become a FOREGONE CONCLUSION!

But if, along the way, you somehow stumble, PROFIT from the experience! Then, vow, by the power of Almighty God, it'll NEVER happen again!

Justice goes on to discuss mental imagery — your "Highlight Reel" — and its importance in establishing both confidence in oneself and in perfecting techniques. If you can see yourself succeeding, you will succeed. Conversely, if all you can do is fail in your thoughts, you have work to do. This "visualization" technique has been used successfully by every champion athlete I have ever known. Justice breaks it down into five simple steps.

Goal setting in sports training is important according to much research. In addition to being motivational, carefully established goals provide you with benchmarks in systematically plotting and acquiring ever-higher levels of skill, strength or endurance. In establishing goals, one must be ever vigilant that they do not limit your upward path. "Even the best can do better," Justice advises. You have to "be "SMART" about it:

SMART usually stands for:

S -- Specific (or Significant).

M -- Measurable (or Meaningful).

A -- Attainable (or Action--Oriented).

R -- Relevant (or Rewarding).

T -- Time--bound (or Track able).

Justice elaborates on short- and long-term goal setting, and exactly how to go about it. He points out that there are four kinds of goals:

- *Outcome Goals (focus on objective results)*

- *Performance Goals (based on past performances)*

- *Process Goals (skills needed)*

- *Results Goals (these cannot be controlled, and often lead to undue pressure)*

I found this section particularly fascinating, as I can't remember ever seeing it so carefully laid out.

Confidence, courage and commitment — the three Cs — are attributes which have strong research support. Justice covers each in minute detail, as he does with the concept of mental toughness. Pressure, personal issues and self-criticism are factored in to one's mental toughness, and Justice covers all of the tried and true coping strategies for each. It is simply amazing how one's mind controls all of these psychological factors, and just as amazing how easily they can be acquired or eliminated. He proposes a five step approach:

1.1.1.   Think carefully about what successes you have, not dwelling on past failures

1.1.2.   Focus your attention to detail

1.1.3.   Regulate your energy through breathing

1.1.4.   Goal setting

1.1.5.   Visualization

A competitive advantage can be gained by sharpening your mental skills, not just your physical attributes. Managing anxiety to razor focus, people skills to positive attitude are covered in detail.

"Mind over head chatter" is part of the book's title. In this section, which I found to be particularly insightful and unique — and hugely important! Self-talk, visualization, relaxation and breathing techniques are methodically addressed with the ultimate goal of getting you "centered" and "in the zone". This attribute, centeredness and in the zone, is often fleeting, rarely mastered and extremely vital to championship level sports performance! Yet, it is achievable, so much so that once mastered, success becomes a foregone conclusion!

Justice explains, "Centering was first designed by sports psychologist Dr. Robert Nideffer and used by Olympic psychologist Dr. Don Greene back in the 1970s. The technique is designed to channel nerves in a productive manner to help the athlete direct focus when encountering any circumstances, and maintain focus, poise, and calm--and quieting the brain's unproductive 'head chatter'."

Well! When I read this, my mind went to the scriptures where it says (more than once), "Be still and know that I am God." Be still, focus! Even in the midst of a storm! ESPECIALLY in the storm of intense competition! For, when you are able to do this, you WILL achieve a peak performance! You will be calm, the mindless head chatter comprised of a veritable flood of competing thoughts of past and future events (sometimes called "the monkey mind") that most people endure throughout their entire lives will cease, leaving you with naught but the task at hand. It is only in the stillness of the NOW moment that this can be accomplished, just as it is the only way to know God. The head chatter is a sure sign that you are not in the present, but are in the past or future, with worry, anger, depression, fear and anxiety. These do not exist in the present moment, and are merely illusory. Now is all you have that's real. THAT is where you must be. THAT is what focus is all about!

Justice elaborates on this important concept:

Mindfulness is paying attention on purpose to the present moment by ignoring distracting thoughts or feelings to your concentration on the present moment. Mindfulness teaches ways to be able to keep all your energy invested in your present moment, rather than having any of it get wasted on trying to get rid of or blocking unwanted thoughts.

Mindfulness can be learned, and Justice elaborates on the steps to achieving it through meditation, learning how to think by overcoming obstacles to thinking (there's a long list of them), and mastering the mind chatter. For me, this was the highlight of this remarkable book!

Justice ended the book with a very moving discussion entitled, "We Are the Champions". Several great athletes are highlighted in his closing section:

Bruce Lee, Wilma Rudolph, Dan Gable, Nadia Comaneci and Michael Jordan.

Said he:

"What perhaps sets great athletes apart is they combined their talents, skills and passions to the nth degree and beyond--showing the world, proving to us that all the beauty, the splendor, the perfection of athletics is indeed humanly possible--and it is possible to have all that wrapped up in a single individual. Maybe the next one could be you."

— Frederick C. Hatfield, Ph.D.
President, International Sports Sciences Association

l

SECTION I

THE DRIVING FORCE — FINDING YOUR MOTIVATION

CHAPTER 1

IGNITING YOUR PASSION

While some say that love makes the world go 'round, for athletes, *passion* is the fuel that inspires positive emotions and higher performance levels. Research shows that it's passion that inspires us with psychological well-being, life satisfaction, and a solid sense of self. This isn't the type of passion found in song lyrics and sultry novels, but rather an essential human attribute that has recently gained more attention in the field of sports psychology.

Passion has traditionally been associated with romantic pursuits, calling to mind hearts and flowers. In reality, however, it's one of the primary ingredients for athletic achievement, and it influences an athlete's ultimate success. Passion is that intense love of the sport, of the game. It's the fuel and the flame – it's the fire deep down in the belly of a champion!

"Firing Up" and Charging

Motivational speakers go to extremes to "fire up" their audiences, using tried and true techniques to inspire and trigger a charge of enthusiasm. But ask any sports performance advisor, and they will tell you that true fire is ignited by a dream, and that dream is fueled by passion. It comes from within, not by listening to others or by observing something.

Dorothy Hamill is an athlete who knows about passion. Critics described her passion as being visually evident in her skating performances. She is one of seven American women to win the Olympic gold medal in figure skating. She's been inducted into both the U.S. and World Figure Skating Hall of Fame. "I remember falling in love with skating the minute I felt that sense of freedom and movement and wind at my face," Hamill said. "I was just passionate about it. I wanted to learn how to skate backward and I wanted to learn how to spin and how to jump."

Sasha Azevedo is a dynamic, multi-talented runner, model, writer, and public speaker. She and other people who are successful in life's endeavors beyond sports are able to use athletics as motivating fuel in their lives. "I run because it's my passion, and not just a sport. Every time I walk out the door, I know why I'm going where I'm going, and I'm already focused on that special place where I find my peace and solitude. Running, to me, is more than just a physical exercise ... it's a consistent reward for victory."

From the Projects to the Pros (The Fuel Behind My Passion)

My parents were the fuel behind my passion. I was taught that no matter what you do in life, give it your best. Growing up in Centerville, a section of projects in Camden, New Jersey, also aided me in having a passion to get out of the neighborhood. Don't get me wrong – of all the places I have lived, without all the neighbors, teammates, school teachers, coaches, and principals, I wouldn't be where I am today. It was truly a community that had pride and didn't settle for anything but the best even in our economic situation (which I didn't know about until I went to the University of Kentucky).

My parents not only put an emphasis on getting out of Camden, but on getting out of the community as a whole. The only means of getting out became part of the fuel for my passion, which meant using my athletic ability to earn a scholarship. That was a known fact to everyone I grew up with.

Being part of a family of five sisters and four brothers, along with many teammates at Camden High, we understood that very well, and we pushed each other. I remember just like it was yesterday how, at the basketball court on 9th and Ferry, you had to earn your right to play with some great ball players in Camden. When I got to high school, I played with teammates such as Little Sonny, Sweet Back, Doc Lee, Boot, Mad Dog, and Smalls. I can go on and on, and I apologize for not being able to mention all the fellas, and how they too had a passion, and how we all pushed each other to the next level. We were South Jersey Football Champs after going 8-0-1, and we won State in basketball as well.

My time in Camden will always be special to me, and is one of the most important parts of my life. Another important part of my passion centered around what was instilled in me from the womb by my mother, which is part of the foundation for my passion. Be respectful, be responsible, and be accountable for my actions. This has carried on throughout my entire life and will continue to do so.

The Power of Passion

According to The Dualistic Model of Passion (Vallerand, 2010), passion is defined as a strong inclination to an activity that is self-defining, that a person loves and finds important, and in which regular time and energy are invested.

Over the past decade, the field of psychology has taken an increased interest in passion. A number of studies have been conducted on the subject and have subsequently led to the publication of professional papers that describe two types of passion – harmonious and obsessive.

Harmonious passion springs from an autonomous internalization of a specific activity into one's identity. It contributes to continuous and ever-expanding psychological well-being. Harmonious passions help prevent negative experiences, like psychological conflicts and the sense of being ill at ease. Other research broadens harmonious passion's outcomes to show that happy people have better health, better relationships, and what notably pertains to sports and athletics, higher levels of performance.

Obsessive passion, on the other hand, springs from a controlled internalization rather than an autonomous one, and it eventually comes to control a person, rather than inspiring or enhancing one's life.

One of the significant factors of harmonious passion is that it involves a person's choice about which activity to pursue, as well as when and how to engage in it. With harmonious passion, the things you love are of value and are actually part of your identity. It is a mindful and open form of the activity.

Researchers believe these results indicate that how people engage in an activity determines the quality of that engagement. How harmonious the passion is for an activity determines the extent of positive benefits accompanying engagement in that activity.

Research has also indicated that with obsessive passion, less than optimal (and even negative) outcomes can be experienced as well.

The obsessively passionate person is uncontrollably engaged in their activity and therefore has difficulty stopping thoughts about it. Performing the activity can lead to conflicts in the person's life in general.

Researchers describe a person with obsessive passion as being "mentally stale," and that this can contribute to burnout. Additionally, this type of passion does not trigger protective functions against uneasiness like harmonious passions do.

With harmonious passion, the person is able to let go of the activity and be fully involved in other life experiences and pursuits without conflict. This is also a protection against burnout.

A great deal of research and support has gone into the "Broaden and Build Theory," which articulates the spiral effect of harmonious passion. The positive effects of harmonious passions lead to ever-increasing (broadening and building) levels of psychological well-being.

Published studies show that benefits of harmonious passion extend beyond the scope of time spent on the actual activity. One particular study that focused on football players revealed that the positive effects of their harmonious passions increased beyond games and practices and lasted throughout the course of an entire season.

All of these studies led them to explain that harmonious passion plays a dual positive role. It leads a person to engage in a passionate activity on a regular basis, and to participate in the desired activity in a way that causes important benefits of emotional and psychological well-being. Harmoniously passionate people engage in their activities with openness and experience activities in a mindful and non-defensive manner. This allows them to reap the positive effects without worrying or dwelling on potential negative outcomes. Furthermore, each harmonious passionate activity has an upward spiral of enduring positive effects – promoting psychological well-being while preventing negative emotions, stress, and tunnel vision. These positive effects of harmonious passion prove valuable to a successful outcome.

Fred Hatfield Talking About Passion

Fred was a mentor, friend, and one of the most passionate people I've ever met. He was one of the first human beings to squat 1000 pounds in competition, and he held three world records in power lifting. He also founded Men's Fitness magazine and was the president of the International Sports Science Association. In the 1980s, he spoke to the Kansas City Chiefs about passion with Art in attendance. A few years ago I interviewed Fred and asked him to talk about that speech. Here's what he said about passion.

"All champions have to begin with passion. Without passion, they're never going to be a champion. They're going to be an also-ran, finishing in second or third. Passion is a hard word to define, which is why you can't put it into somebody yourself – you have to help them find it within themselves. All I can do, instead of telling you what passion is, is to tell you what passion is not.

Passion is not your need to achieve; instead, it's a burning desire to exceed all bounds.

It is not commitment to excellence; it's utter disdain for anything less.

It's not endless hours of practice; it's perfect practice.

It's not your ability to cope, either. It's the total domination of every situation in life. You don't cope – you overwhelm.

It's not setting unrealistic or vague goals – because goals, all too often, prescribe performance limits.

It's not doing what it takes to win. It's doing what it takes to exceed the bounds of mere convention.

It's not the force, skill, or muscle. Rather, it's the explosive, often calamitous, force of will.

Now, if you believe in and practice these things, then for you, winning is neither everything nor the only thing, as Vince Lombardi used to say. For you, winning is a foregone conclusion. You know you're going to win. You planned it that way, and you make it so. If along the way you stumble, sometimes we all do that. Profit from the experience, but then vow, by the power given to you by almighty God, it's never going to happen again."

Goal Attainment, Passion, and Well-Being

Accomplishing a goal feels great. For many people, achieving a goal brings feelings of well-being and happiness. Conversely, many people typically feel let down when they fail to succeed or reach a goal.

When it comes to athletics, however, there is a special benefit of passion that works to protect psychological well-being following failures that are related to that passionate activity. People who have harmonious passion exhibit a secure sense of self that lets them handle setbacks in a mindful and non-defensive way. People who operate out of obsessive passion, though, may suffer negative impacts from setbacks because they are obsessive about maintaining their identity and sense of self-esteem.

Professional sports are all about goals and winning. But even the best of the best know they cannot hit a home run every time they come up to bat, or always cross the finish line first. Harmonious passion helps an athlete to better deal with life's inevitable defeats – on and off the field.

Fuel for Thought

For those who feel the need to rekindle their charge of passion, and for those who want to help young people develop and open up to their passion, health professionals and creativity experts across the board offer suggested activities that are helpful.

- Revisit the positive events of your childhood and focus on the activities and pastimes you enjoyed.

- Make your "passion poster" or "creativity board" and put your thoughts into words or a collage of images, articles, poems, and other inspirations. When you surround yourself with messages and images of what you believe, what your intentions are, and declarations about who you want to become, your awareness and passion will grow along with your vision of where you are, and anything that is missing gets filled in to make your vision a reality.

If you fear or feel paralyzed about moving into what could be your passion, shift out of this mode by listing some of the people who are where you'd like to be. Read up on them and find something that resonates with you about what they said. Some new ideas may even sprout from reading about their life.

What Do the Pros Say?

My high school wrestling coach used to say, "Embrace the grind." Coaches will usually tell you that an athlete who has passion loves to train. One coach said it's like their passion is part of their DNA. They ease through their challenges.

Another coach said that some athletes may complain about doing "two-a-day workouts" during football season under the hot sun, but they just do it and appreciate all the hard work that it takes to be successful. They don't have to love every second, but their heart and motivation is propelled by their passion. They know they've just got to take the bumps along their path to greatness. They can quickly move through tough times and be ready for the next day.

Another coach described how athletes without passion show up with "holes in their games" during challenging times, like when there's a slump or some type of pressure or stressful situation. They may even start to blame their teammates, coaches, referees, and even the weather when things aren't going their way.

Sports psychologists also affirm that for a passionate athlete, stress and failure are actually part of the mind's system of understanding and accounting. They are able to quickly and successfully deal with these challenges. Psychologists describe these athletes as having an obvious devotion and love for their training, besides simply being naturally talented.

Talent vs. Passion – Striking a Balance

Gymnast Kirk Mango is a national champion, a three-time All-American, and a Hall of Fame athlete. Records show that when he was younger, he was not very talented. He stuck with it because he was passionate about it, and it paid off.

While both talent and passion can work for an individual in his or her pursuits, the amount of passion and devotion is usually a good indication of an athlete's longevity and long-term success in the sport.

One sports psychologist summed this up with a favorite quote for athletes: "The only thing you deserve is what you earn." In other words, passionate athletes learn from challenges and setbacks and use them as building blocks with no excuses.

Passion as Protection

Another benefit of harmonious passion is that it has been shown to protect an athlete from experiencing more serious physical injuries. Studies determined that the more passionate you are about your sport, the less likely you are to be severely injured. Why? Those with harmonious passion tend to be in peak physical shape, which generally helps to minimize their risk of sustaining general injuries, and because of their positive passion about their sport, they are less prone to engage in risky behavior. They're more likely to take it easy and allow themselves to recuperate when injured, so that they don't risk a chronic injury. The person with harmonious passion is in control of an activity and exhibits flexible persistence that helps avoid risk of chronic injury.

Now that you have learned a bit about the power of individual passion, the next chapter will discuss how success is a team effort, on and off the field of play!

CHAPTER 2

SUCCESS IS A TEAM EFFORT - YOUR SUPPORT SYSTEMS AND INFLUENCES

To paraphrase a line from 16th century poet John Donne, "No man or woman is an island." This adage applies to all athletes, regardless of whether they take part in team or individual sports. Athletes often credit (or complain about) their interactions and experiences with family, friends, instructors, coaches, teammates, and sports psychologists. For athletes, this network of resources serves to help their mind and body perform at optimal levels, it plays an important role in their day-to-day routine, and ultimately their successes and failures. And research explores the strong influence of all these support systems on sports enthusiasts and athletes.

From the Projects to the Pros (Building A Team)

Growing up in the 60s and 70s meant there were likely some serious racial tensions, regardless of where you lived. Camden, New Jersey, where I lived and attended school, was a predominantly African-American and Puerto Rican community. My mother taught us there are different shades of people, and you treat others with respect regardless of shade.

Steve Koche was my 5th grade teacher, a white guy from the suburbs that saw something in me despite our differences in appearance. He would pick me up in his Triumph TR6 to play basketball with his white friends that played at the college level, and they would give me encouragement, along with tips to improve my game. We still talk on a daily basis, and if I'm in New Jersey, we hang out – likewise if he's in Kansas City. We have been best of friends for about 50 years now, and it's beyond that – we are family. Steve was and continues to be the perfect role model for me (except his driving abilities, because he drives like Mr. Magoo).

Reverend Charlie Dawson, who we called Brother Dawson, was another individual who was great not only for me but my entire family. He was the preacher at the Broadway Bible Tabernacle, and every Sunday morning and evening service along with prayer meeting on Wednesday is where we would be. The Warrens, Roziers, Drummonds, Gilberts and Sister Ruth were some of the people who created this unique extended family dynamic. One person from my community that made a name for himself in football was Mike Rosier.

Brother Dawson used to be a heavyweight boxer. His whole life centered around doing the right thing in every aspect of his life – how you eat, exercise, help others, and so on. He took all of the young ones, especially the boys, and talked to us about doing what was right. His sermons back up that message too, and as I stated earlier he lived what he preached. There were times when he would take me and my other three brothers to his home in the country where we would help him work outside. He would provide instructions and then work side by side with us. He set a fine example for us and taught us to do what you say and say what you do, and that will forever be appreciated. What you saw in him is what you got. A great man!

On Sundays, after the morning services, my brothers, Wendell, Gary, Dennis, and I would go religiously (no pun intended) to the Rescue Mission where the Bible was taught, and afterwards was the best part – CANDY! Mr. Frank Wallin, who was part of it, took a special interest in us. Much like Steve Koch, Mr. Frank was a white guy who lived in the suburbs. His wife, three sons, and daughter would invite Wendell and me to their house for the weekend on occasion. It was a little different at first, but we were always accepted as part of their family. I can remember playing various sports, watching television, and doing all sorts of things together as a family. These were truly special times that taught me some important lessons. One is that just because you didn't come out of the same womb, or are a different shade, from a different part of town, or don't have a fancy house, car, or that you are short, tall, wear glasses, are slim, heavy set, doesn't exempt you from being family. After leaving Camden, we fell out of touch and haven't spoken in over forty years. Recently, Mr. Frank's son, Andy, contacted me via Facebook. When we finally talked, it brought back that positive family bond that has helped make me the person I am today. Mr. Frank is now in his 80s, and I'm truly thankful that I got a chance to talk to him and express how appreciative I was for all of his and his family's support during my formative years.

Now, if you want to talk about characters, I welcome you to my Uncle Eddie and Uncle Peaches. They lived in Sheldon Terrace, the project next to us. Uncle Eddie was in the war and only had one leg, but it didn't hold him back. Looking back, they were true entrepreneurs. They both took an interest in my brothers and me, along with others in the neighborhood, and were all about helping others. They would emphasize to all the young ones the importance of getting an education, respecting your parents, and doing something positive in the neighborhood. Their actions backed up what they preached. One of the many things they did was create the Centerville Runners, a neighborhood youth basketball team. Keep in mind, I don't think their background was in basketball, but they gave it their all. They bought our jerseys and scheduled games with other teams in the suburbs that made me feel like I was a part of something special before I even got to Camden High School. We would have snacks and drinks after the game and get together just to hang out, away from a lot of the negative things going on. This was a bond that shaped me. Their actions helped me appreciate the importance of taking an interest in others and doing as much as I can to help out when possible.

Studies Support the Value of Support Systems

The U.S. Olympic Committee recently conducted a survey of past champions that focused on the various factors related to their success. A 57% majority attributed their success to the emotional and financial support of family and friends. Positive relationships also ranked as a top factor in the success of these champions, instilling these world-class athletes with confidence and stability. Not far behind was the 49% who credited their success to excellent coaches throughout their development. Additionally, 22% credited success to their individualized training programs and access to top-notch facilities.

On the other hand, these Olympians indicated the top obstacles they had overcome in the past included a lack of coaching expertise, insufficient support from coaches, and personal conflicts with members of the coaching staff. They also revealed that a significant deterrent to success was a lack of support by family, friends, and peers, who discouraged their athletic pursuits.

Many other studies confirm these results as well – talented athletes need the unconditional support of the people in their lives, regardless of whether the athletes are winning at any given time. From data collected, interpreters of the Olympic survey explained that coaches, and the quality of support athletes receive from their coaches, are a critical influence throughout the course of an athlete's development.

Coaches Can Make Champions, But What Makes a Great Coach?

The Olympic Committee's survey shed light on the specific characteristics top athletes felt were most important in a coach. The survey revealed the best kind of coaching support includes being knowledgeable, motivating, dedicated, committed, and encouraging. The Olympic survey further explained that coaches must keep in mind that every player is unique. Therefore, a great coach needs to recognize the range of factors most significant for an individual athlete's success, and to know just how to communicate the specific training needs to that unique athlete. A great coach recognizes and values the major influence they have on their athletes. A great coach also works relentlessly to develop vital coaching skills and constantly tailors those skills according to the needs of each athlete.

Interpreters of the Olympic survey then posed two vital questions for coaches to ask themselves in order to provide optimal support to their athletes:

1. What pieces are in place that will go into the continued development of that athlete's talent?

2. What are the roadblocks the athlete must knock down with the coach's help?

During interviews, Olympic coaches revealed the process of their own coaching methods. One coach described some effective techniques in this way: "I allow them to speak first, make sure I am available. I pay attention to body language, and make sure I say something to each player. I can be blunt, honest. I tell each player that I want them to get better." One of this particular coach's players added that her coach knows and loves the game, gives it everything, values her opinion, and is open, receptive, and organized. She said, "We as athletes want to know the coach has control, but can be dominant when required with honest feedback, steady with a questioning and listening approach, influencing with encouragement and praise."

The involved and passionate coach who gives it everything is far from a new concept, of course. Everson Walls, former Grambling State University and NFL cornerback, said about Coach Eddie G. Robinson, "Coach Rob, he did a lot more for us than teach us about football. He used to come through the halls early in the morning with a cowbell, waking us up for class and for church."

Great coaches often find themselves having to pick up a cowbell of sorts and ring it loud and clear (not a literal one, like Coach Robinson, but metaphorical). Think of it this way – a vital component of a coach's role is to serve as the voice of reason and clarity when the athletes under his or her care start getting distracted and discouraged by the thoughts and perceived messages in their own heads. Let's call this "head chatter," that destructive inner voice that tells a person he or she isn't good enough. Self-awareness and mastery coach Gary van Warmerdam describes it like this: "For most people, the mind has developed into something that does incessant describing, comparing, and judging." Head chatter only brings an athlete down. It's up to a great coach to help an athlete cut through that chatter and stay focused.

The Wizard of Westwood's Mastery Climate for Success

John Wooden, a basketball Hall of Fame player and coach, developed a program that focuses on continually striving for excellence. Rather than placing the focus on winning, his coaching plan creates "a mastery-oriented motivational climate." It's a recipe for success that is followed by many coaches and recognized by sports psychologists as providing an environment of helpful support and a system for athletic achievement. In this supportive type of coaching climate, the focus is on fostering growth in the player, both as an athlete and a person. The emphasis is on doing what it takes for peak performance, not on winning – putting one's best efforts toward learning, improving, and attaining goals. In this environment, winning is secondary to enjoying the sport, and an athlete continually improves his or her skills at the same time. It's an atmosphere of mutual support and encouragement, one that recognizes each athlete's importance both as an individual and to the team.

Surveys and studies of those involved with mastery climates show that positive relationships between coach and athlete lead to increased enjoyment of the sport, better team cohesion, and better self-esteem experienced by the athletes. In mastery climates, not only is there reduced anxiety and fear of failure, but a reduction in dropout rates for the athletes as well.

Support from "Sports Shrinks" is Growing

Over the years, in addition to coaches and athletes, sports psychologists have become increasingly involved in sports. More and more, competitive athletes are turning to professional sports psychologists for assistance in a range of challenges and problems including communication, motivation, control, mental strategizing, and for help dealing with pressures from family, coaches, expectations, injury, and recovery.

Various levels of credentials exist for sports psychologists. Athletes who seek the expertise of a sports psychologist should find one who is a member of a professional organization, such as the APA and the Association for Applied Sports Psychology. Many sports psychologists are licensed psychologists with specific post-doctorate training in optimizing performance and well-being. A spotlight shined on the role of the sports psychologist when NBA finals hero Ron Artest of the Los Angeles Lakers made an unexpected public statement following the game when he thanked "everybody in my hood... my doctor... my psychiatrist. There's so much commotion going on in the playoffs. She helped me relax."

Dr. Nicole Miller, a sports psychology consultant with the U.S. Olympic team, noted that sports psychologists are assisting athletes at an increasing rate, especially with challenges related to underlying anger issues and teaching breathing techniques, as well as methods of positive self-talk. Supportive instruction like this increases athletic performance.

According to sports psychologists who work with the U.S. Army, athletes (and soldiers) can only achieve peak performance when they understand the dynamic of "family functioning" and view the team as a family. On the team, the athletes are not just battle buddies, but members of a family with conflicts to deal with, just like any other family. What's most important, the Army's sports psychologists felt, is for athletes to know how to manage the inevitable conflicts.

These professionals described their roles as making sure the athletes in their care got a chance to express their feelings and learn how to rally around each other for support and group cohesion. They monitored how athletes set goals and encouraged realistic expectations. These sports psychologists helped athletes recognize the potential for over-stimulation or under-stimulation, and they explained that both lead to wasted energy. Their jobs included helping athletes recognize that energy and direct it where it's needed instead.

Psychological Training

If you're an athlete, you know the value of physical activity and sport-specific training. Now, consider this: you can train your brain for optimal psychological performance as well.

There are specific sports psychology programs available for sports enthusiasts at all levels. One such program is called Psychological Skills Training, or PST. In this program, skills that athletes develop include goal setting, self-talk, mental imagery, mental rehearsal, confidence boosting, coping with the pressures of high-level competition, letting go of mistakes, exposing perfectionist traits, and relaxation. Athletes often credit their success to the support they received from technique-boosting programs like this. Take Matt Boni, for example, who moved from amateur motocross champion at age 15 to pro motocross racer.

Sports psychologists point to how their field enables athletes to gain success in the pursuit of goals and in the enjoyment of their sport. Psychological training promotes balance for the athlete, both in the sport itself and in the rest of the athlete's life, including areas like family and interaction with coaches, officials, and other participants.

Research confirms that supportive coaching is not just about knowing the sport and teaching required physical and mental skills. Supportive coaching is also about being in tune with the athletes, knowing what is going on with them physically and emotionally in order to provide the support they need. Sometimes, athletes experience burnout. A supportive coach recognizes the symptoms of impending burnout – low energy, extra irritability, attitude problems, unusual complaining, not enjoying the sport, and poor performance. Supportive coaches deal with burnout using a variety of methods, such as being flexible in general program procedures, modeling passion and enthusiasm, placing emphasis on the process rather than the outcome, and scheduling breaks (and even vacation days) from training.

As Vince Lombardi said, "Coaches who win get inside their players and motivate. Athletes need to believe in you, see and feel your passion, know you are there for them, that they are your priority." No sports enthusiast or athlete can go it alone. Once he or she recognizes his or her passion and begins to seek a trainer, the athlete will need a trainer who is passionate about the sport, who models it, who communicates well, and who has the knowledge both to teach and to inspire.

The Collaboration for Sports Performance

All the experts agree that success at any given sport requires a systematic team approach, even for individual athletic competitions!

A successful sport system is a collaborative team effort between the athlete, coach, family, and friends. Every factor that can and does affect performance contributes to the system, such as emotional and financial stability. Out of a successful sports system comes the high-performance athlete.

High-performance athletes exhibit flow. Flow is described by psychologists as the mental state in which a person performing an activity is totally immersed in a feeling of energized focus. In studies on the subject, athletes were interviewed, and their responses indicated the myriad factors that affect an athlete's flow. Flow performances were described as the results of teamwork, active verbal and emotional support from coaches, emotional support from other athletes, and emotional and technical assistance from supplemental expert support staff.

To high-performance athletes, success is the result of far more than personal factors. The best of the best exhibit mastery of the sport, and mastery can only occur within a supportive environment. Supportive environments encompass trained, functioning, and coordinated personnel and resources such as organization support staff. This is true at every level of athletics, from the local high school to the big leagues. High-performance athletes are most likely to recognize their full potential for athletic success when they come from this kind of supportive environment.

The Role of Parents

By the time an athlete becomes "world famous," or even notably successful, mom and dad might seem invisible. But research shows that high-performance athletes usually had positive developmental experiences and were subjected to plenty of positive reinforcement from their parents during their formative years.

Through the support of their parents, athletes learn about the value of persistence. Parents are often the ones who select the young athlete's coach, with or without the child's input. Research on parental involvement found that high-performance athletic achievements stem from parents who offered their offspring emotional and financial support, along with coaches who worked to both prepare the athlete for (and buffer him or her from) adverse influences in training and competition. As the athletes developed and their careers advanced, this level of parent/coach support continued to play a role in the face of increasing challenges. The support of parents and coaches helped to confirm past experiences of athletic prowess, as well as to acknowledge increasing capabilities at each level of performance. Several high-profile athletes interviewed during this study explained that their mastery of the sport and their coping skills against stress were due to their past experiences within support systems that started with mom and dad and continued throughout their careers as members of a team.

Team Studies, Group Dynamics & Cohesion

Team building is a popular subject in sports psychology research and textbooks. What athletes know intuitively, that a good team is necessary to win competitions, is described in depth throughout recent studies.

A number of researchers have focused on group dynamics, which are defined as the interaction of individuals who assist, and rely on each other to accomplish a mutual task. This research identifies that where there's a group, there is likely cohesion. However, cohesion can occur regardless of how well the individuals like one another. A group can be bound by their tasks, affection, and respect for one other, or conversely, can be bound by their tasks and their dislike for one another. Interestingly, either case can lead to success of the team.

Case in point: the 1978 New York Yankees were well known for not getting along with one another, but they also exhibited amazing task cohesion. With a record of 100-63, they won their third consecutive American League pennant.

Researchers describe highly cohesive groups as being united and committed to success. Team cohesion is based on the concerns and beliefs held by the individual members about the team, such as what attracted them to the team in the first place. One study revealed it is a threat to team cohesion when teams lean too heavily on outstanding individuals rather than functioning as a collective. Simply put, teams who are overly reliant on talented divas do not perform as well. Teams composed of more modest individuals were shown to be more likely to exceed expectations. This research points to the role of the coach in building a team that performs well with interdependent members.

This isn't to say, however, that a coach cannot put together a cohesive team with star players. Coaches just need to tend to the task of fostering cohesion and helping team members put their individual strengths toward the purpose of something larger. And it's not the outcome of the game – research shows that the effort and process involved in team building result in cohesion and more success than when teams focus on winning each game. Researchers believe that winning will take care of itself with a cohesive team.

Research on team building points to the following as dependable aspects of team cohesion:

1. A clear role defined for team individuals

2. Willingness on the part of individuals to make personal sacrifices for the team

3. Quality communication between members

4. Shared goals

The Supportive Team Climate

Researchers correlate team climate to the value judgments held by team players. Team members describe these components of a strong team climate as: some autonomy, a good balance of stress and the pressure to succeed without being pushed beyond limits, motivation to aspire to new heights, fairness, and desire to be on the team.

Summarizing Effective Team Traits

To recap, the players, coaches, and sports psychologists involved in recent research on team effectiveness sum up the essential components of effective team dynamics. A cohesive team has the following attributes:

- Coaches and athletes who give of themselves to team efforts

- Clear expectations for roles

- Effective communication strategies

- Respect for everyone

- Viewing the team as greater than the sum of its parts (i.e. team over individual member)

- Celebrating individual differences and contributions

- Recognition of outstanding behavior and role performance

- Including everyone in the process of setting team goals

- Providing feedback that maximizes learning and encourages activity outside routine practice

The Secret Weapon

Confidence. There's no doubt that on game days, an athlete's confidence provides the ultimate competitive edge. A high-performance athlete's confidence can be seen as the natural outcome of the factors that comprise his or her support system. From initial training and competition to career advancement and continued success, an athlete who gets support from his or her network of resources is confident and unstoppable.

How to Develop Strong Support

Here are a few tips for an athlete creating a system of support:

- Share your goals and plans with your family and ask for their help and encouragement

- Hire a coach who can understand what you are going through and is invested in your personal success

- Find a training partner at your level or even more advanced who can encourage and cheer you on

- Join a group or find new friends with similar goals

- Encourage others to perform their best results in them doing the same for you

Physical Support

Nutrition:

You are what you eat, and there are numerous official programs that provide nutritional support to athletes to ensure they adopt the best nutritional strategies for performance. Dietary assessment can evaluate an athlete's food intake to spot deficiencies and formulate plans to maximize performance and weight manipulation. Dietary plans take into consideration travel or special environments, health, and medical issues.

Physiotherapy:

Sports medicine practitioners include physiotherapists that provide support through assessment and management of conditions affecting the muscles and skeletal system. This may involve rehabilitation, manipulation, exercises, and soft tissue treatment. The sports physician is a specialist in sports medicine with a broad understanding of physiology, medicine, anatomy, psychology, psychiatry, and pathology who takes a holistic view of an athlete.

Supporting it All

While the term "athletic supporter" may call to mind an entirely different image, the fact is that no athlete, professional or amateur, can go it alone. It's been said it takes a village to raise a child, but for an athlete to reach his or her ultimate success, it takes a comprehensive support system. This is where champions come from. As said by Mia Hamm, National Soccer Hall of Famer and a FIFA World Player of the Year, "I am a member of a team, and I rely on the team, I defer to it and sacrifice for it, because the team, not the individual, is the ultimate champion."

CHAPTER 3

WHAT MAKES A CHAMPION?

The word "champion" has more than a nice ring to it. A person fortunate enough to be called a champion has got it all – past, present, and future. Champions are the epitome of admiration and respect. What does it take to become a champion? Are there specific paths and provisions? Or is it just about luck?

Is it about all of the above, or something else?

Are Champions Born or Made?

Muhammad Ali, one of the greatest champions of all time, answered those questions with this quote: "Champions aren't made in the gyms. Champions are made from something they have deep inside them – a desire, a dream, a vision."

Dan Bell, who coached thousands of athletes over the course of his career – including multiple Olympians – offered some insight about the hearts and souls of champions verses everyone else. Coach Bell said, "Of course, there are the expected genetics, luck, and talent. But the operative word is 'boredom.'"

This may not be what you'd expect to hear regarding champions, but Bell went on to explain, "It comes down to who can handle the boredom of training every day and doing the same lifts over and over and over again."

Some athletes will get depressed when they lose focus or motivation, believing they just don't have what those other successful champs have – some inborn, unstoppable passion, willpower, or magic pill. But as Coach Bell vouched, all successful athletes feel the same boredom and lack of motivation that everyone else feels. Those top performers, though, show up and work through the boredom. They embrace the daily grind of practice that's required to reach their goals. They stick to their goals through action without letting their emotions steer them off course. They work when the work isn't easy, and they work even when they aren't motivated or inspired. They know it isn't about a single event, but an overall commitment to the process. These top performers are true champions, not different because of their achievements. They are in love with their own process of doing it, of doing the daily practice, not just the individual event.

These top performers have fallen in love with building identities for themselves as people doing the work, not just dreaming of the results they'd like. Thus, results take care of themselves.

In his book, "The Gift: A Runner's Story," Paul Maurer describes his take based on his own experiences. "Running isn't a sport for pretty boys," Maurer writes. "It's about the sweat in your hair and the blisters on your feet. It's the frozen spit on your chin and the nausea in your gut. It's about throbbing calves and cramps at midnight that are strong enough to wake the dead. It's about getting out the door and running when the rest of the world is only dreaming about having the passion that you need to live each and every day with. It's about being on a lonely road and running like a champion even when there's not a single soul in sight to cheer you on. Running is all about having the desire to train and persevere until every fiber in your legs, mind, and heart is turned to steel. And when you've finally forged hard enough, you will have become the best runner you can be. And that's all that you can ask for."

Champions, as runner and author Maurer explained, live a lifestyle motivated by a passion for excellence in everything they do. Champions experience every activity or task as an opportunity (or a challenge) to set new goals and to try to achieve new things. These athletes have a way of doing everything not by asking how to do it or if they can do it, but how to do it well and better than expected.

A champion is the athlete who feels driven to venture outside his comfort zone. A champion is comfortable with accepting discomfort as a challenge to do more, to go harder, to make an extra sacrifice, to not be satisfied with just a good job, but for the edge, the better way, the new angle, whatever it takes. This is what separates the champion from the rest. It's not talent or advantages. Champions see hard work as opportunity – a stepping stone toward goals and dreams – without being swayed by what's going on around them.

Quotes from noteworthy coaches and players reiterate these ideas.

"Never let the fear of striking out get in your way. I swing big, with everything I've got. I hit big or I miss big. I like to live as big as I can."
—Babe Ruth

"To be a champion, you have to learn to handle stress and pressure. But if you've prepared mentally and physically, you don't have to worry."
—Harvey McKay

"There's always the motivation of wanting to win. Everybody has that. But a champion needs, in his attitude, a motivation above and beyond winning."

—Pat Riley

"Which player is mentally stronger? Which player is going to fight the hardest in the big points? These are the things that determine who is the champion."

—Novak Djokovic

"I hated every minute of training, but I said, 'Don't quit. Suffer now and live the rest of your life as a champion.'"

—Muhammad Ali

Finally, from athlete and political achiever Arnold Schwarzenegger, "The last three or four reps is what makes the muscle grow. This area of pain divides the champion from someone else who is not a champion. That's what most people lack, having the guts to go on and just say they'll go through the pain no matter what happens."

From the Projects to the Pros – A Disciplined Approach

When most people think of being a champion, it generally has to do with a sport.

When I think of a champion, the first people who come to mind are my parents, particularly my mother. Her vision, heart, and soul were devoted to creating an environment for my siblings and me to thrive and be able to "fish" on our own in this world.

This was reflected in everything she did. I didn't have to have my eyes open to see it. I could smell and taste it by the way she prepared our meals, always well-balanced, and we sat together as a family to eat. She also set the example of a healthy lifestyle by the way she lived. She did not smoke, drink, or pollute her mind and heart with vocabulary that isn't found in the dictionary.

She also taught us the importance of structure. We went to bed at a specific time and got up at a specific time. She made sure that we had plenty of rest. We were also taught to be respectful. We were properly disciplined. This was another aspect of my mother's vision, that we were responsible and accountable for our actions.

There were four of us boys who were all born within two years of each other. We came to know what discipline was on a daily basis. Although we were very slow learners, we understood what discipline and punishment meant.

My mother wouldn't hesitate to line us up and hand out physical punishment when necessary. This is where I developed the psychological part of what has helped me throughout my life and in sports. I wasn't as worried about the physical pain of being spanked as I was making sure that I was first. It was a mental game to me, visualizing the end result and getting it over first to see my brothers get their turn. In my mind, this gave me the edge. Thinking back on it, this may have been the beginning of my visualization, which we will discuss in the next chapter.

Starting from the End Result

Coaches and others involved in the leadership and business side of running teams all agree: talent is hardly the only thing needed to be a champion. When these leaders list the qualities that make the best of the best different from other talented individuals, they find some common denominators. Then from this list, the coaches can determine what skills need to be improved upon for an individual athlete's ultimate success.

One coach determined the first ingredient to be "teachability." He explained that for an athlete to develop talent, he or she must be able to consistently and perpetually learn, relearn, and even unlearn if necessary. The coach described the archetypal champion as a sponge with water rather than a rock in water. He explained the unfortunate scenario of an exceptionally talented athlete who becomes a know-it-all and ceases to absorb new knowledge. He contrasted this hypothetical "stunted athlete" with Olympians who become serial champions as they continue learning and reinventing how they can win. Real life champions that fit this description include cyclist Sir Chris Hoy, rower Sir Steve Redgrave, and sailor Ben Ainslie.

The second ingredient is playing under pressure. A champion with this characteristic learns to be comfortable in the stress of the moment without choking, freezing, or bottling up. It is a process of learning through experiences which develops this ability. Many times, great golfers are older when they have learned to come to grips with the final day's intense pressure. One coach explained that, similar to the military technique of planning for all possible scenarios before going into battle, athletes need to spend enough time planning, talking, and mentally preparing before getting out there not only to play, but to be ready as well. Another coach walked his rugby team through moves in very slow motion so that each player could visualize what needed to be done and where on the field everyone would be.

The third ingredient is attitude, and a champion's attitude is really a combination of six components:

1. Passion: having intense emotions for the game. The playing is done every day because of an immense desire to do so.

2. Dedication: a total commitment to the goal that endures through flawed and painful days. This remains through the good times and the bad.

3. Confidence: belief that one has the ability, power, self-reliance, and assurance that he or she can do it.

4. Drive, Determination, and Discipline: something that pushes a champion to succeed or excel. It's a motivating ingredient.

5. Authentic Vision: having a self-understanding of what he or she wants, and knowing how to anticipate what can or will come to be.

6. Respect: holding a sense of worth and excellence about oneself as well as a genuine respect for others as well.

The Sports Psychologist Reports

A report delivered to the 2012 Pre-Olympic Scientific Convention revealed the study's investigation of the value of training compared to the genetic factors that contribute to turning a talented athlete into a champion. Sports science refers to champions as "elite performance" athletes. This particular report addressed the question of whether champions are born or made. The authors of this study concluded that both training and environmental factors are critical for elite performance; however, without taking genetic factors into account, they would not be able to account for an elite athlete. Deliberate practice can improve both physical skills and psychological performance to a significant extent. But expert performance cannot be guaranteed by training and practice alone because there are differences in genetics that are also crucial to performance in sports that inevitably come into play with training.

This review further concluded that it is genetic makeup that will first determine certain performance thresholds; training is a subsequent process that can optimize genetic potential. The study illuminated the components of genetic influences on performance, describing several physiological and biochemical systems and pathways which interact and must work at the most optimal levels to produce elite performance.

The Complex Body

Everyone's body is complex. Consider all the interactions of your musculoskeletal, cardiovascular, central nervous, and respiratory systems. In sports, this complexity takes on additional significance since individual sports utilize the various body systems in different ways. For example, an athlete requiring endurance and an athlete requiring sprinting or quick bursts of power will have different advantages and face different challenges based on how their bones and muscles respond to the rigors of their individual sports.

Going deeper into the biology and chemistry of the body further shows how complex the body is with its different cells, proteins, macromolecules, and coding genes. Therefore, identifying components that can determine superior athletic performance is complex and elusive.

The extensive 2012 pre-Olympic study discussed the following physical attributes which contribute to elite performance: VO2 max trainability, sex, height, and skeletal muscle properties.

VO2 max has to do with a person's maximum ability to use oxygen during intense physical activity. It is measured in milliliters of oxygen (O2) per unit of body weight. The greater your VO2 max threshold, the stronger your stamina and endurance. VO2 max traits are reported to be heritable, and this has been proven in chromosome testing results. Researchers determined that some of these chromosomes have a very powerful influence on an individual's training and performance.

World records in track and field show that the best male athletes outperform the best female athletes. However, the women's marathon world record is above the top performances in history. This is one good reason that men and women complete in separate categories.

Height is more complex than sex because it is a combination of several environmental factors, including nutrition, growth, and development. Height is an essential attribute for some sports like basketball and volleyball, but would be considered a negative quality for success in sports such as endurance running.

Skeletal and muscle tissue respond positively to exercise. As a category, skeletal muscle includes muscle mass and strength, muscle power, and metabolism. Muscle mass and strength has been proven to be partly genetic, but more research is needed to substantiate the roles that both genetics and environment play in terms of muscle anaerobic power.

Possibilities and Performance Abilities

More recent research has reported that exercise, and various techniques and forms of exercise, can create changes that lead to better memory and better mechanisms for coping with stress, which can and does affect training and athletic performance abilities.

The researchers offer that a correct combination of intrinsic genetic factors can determine who will be a talented athlete, but to become an elite athlete, one has to experience the correct combination of other external factors, and there can be many potential possibilities that determine that outcome. For example, external factors can result in injuries, illness, or burnout.

So does all of this mean the potential to be a champion is in your genes? And if you don't have those athletic genetic factors, why bother to train as hard as you can, through all the pain and monotony like all those coaches and champions said was necessary? The answer to the first question is, no one has been able to identify an exact "champion gene." Besides, no matter what your genetic destiny is, you can achieve whatever full potential is locked in your DNA. This only happens, though, if you train and think like a champion.

Common Characteristics of Champions

Dr. Marissa Adviento, sports psychologist and part-time faculty member at Ateneo de Manila University, conducted a 2012 study of five top world-ranking Filipino athletes that revealed they shared six common characteristics. It is worth noting that these six are similar to those mentioned earlier in the study that specified six essential attitude characteristics. Each of the elite athletes in this particular study achieved top rankings in their sport.

The first common characteristic is passion — the enjoyment, the love that never wears off regardless of the number of years devoted to it. One athlete commented he was "too crazy" about bowling.

The second characteristic was described as a tenacious striving for perfection, uncompromising in their commitment to excellence and in perfecting their respective crafts, despite setbacks, despite all the ups and downs.

The third characteristic is discipline and determination. The dedicated approach to their sport drove them to exceed body limits and sacrifice pastimes and pleasures for training. They welcomed opportunities to compete with better players.

The fourth characteristic is authenticity. These elite athletes were all well aware of both their strengths and limitations, both in their sports and in their personal lives. They offered a picture of a true self without covering up flaws or weaknesses.

The fifth characteristic is goal orientation, both in their sport and in their life goals as well. These athletes took pride in other lifestyle pursuits apart from their sport specific goals.

The sixth characteristic is a positive outlook. Each was able to see adversity and any setbacks as learning opportunities to from which to grow. Setbacks never stopped these champions, including personal setbacks such as one who endured despite marital problems. Rather than succumb to depression, one of the athletes chose to think of his losses as an unfortunate twist of fate.

Dr. Adviento concluded that there is a champion mindset that allows the athletes to push themselves relentlessly, like heroes on a quest, toward their goals.

Anyone Can Be a Champion

The qualities that make a champion are not reserved for the lucky or the chosen. A champion does not have to bring home the gold medal, win the tournament, or make newspaper headlines. All the qualities that have been studied and discussed reveal that a champion's character is composed of attributes anyone can have.

Consider the following quote by an anonymous champion. She's a lover of a sport, but not famous, and she described herself so well, like many other sports enthusiasts would describe themselves.

"I'm a high school player. I'm a team player. I play with my friends and with some of my enemies, but I respect everyone when it comes to my sport. I know I'm not going to get a multi-million-dollar contract to play professionally. I know I may not even get my name in the paper. I play for love of the game. For the pride and honor, for the blood, sweat and tears it takes to make the team, to earn the spot, to win the game. I play because I can; I play because I know that my life would be empty without the sport I play. I would have a lack of everything my sport gives me... integrity, courage, talent, fearlessness, pride, strength, stamina, will and the heart of a champion. If I didn't play, I would lose a part of me. I'm an athlete. I'm a girl. I'm a champion. Not because my team always wins, but because when we don't we learn from our mistakes. We try to fix them, and most of all because we have fun. I have built lifelong friendships and memories because of my being an athlete. I leave everything on the field or court and continue to push myself. I

am never happy with second place, but I have learned to accept it. I have learned to get over and through my anger and be the athlete and player I have always dreamed of being. I don't play for my parents, for my family, for my friends; I don't play for my coach or my teachers or my school. I play for myself, but when I'm playing I represent them. It isn't about winning or losing, but I hate to lose. I won't settle for a tie, and I am not satisfied with 100%. To play, you have to sacrifice everything, your body, your time, your sweat, blood and tears, everything for your team. I am a player, and athlete and a champion, not because I know what it is like to win, but because I know what it is like to lose. I know what it is like to feel the anger and pain that comes along with second best. I have been that girl with tears in her eyes, walking out to receive the second place trophy and clapping as the other team, my opponents, receive the first place one. I know what it is like to lose, to win, to want to quit, to want to cry, to not want to get up. I know what it is like to hear the cheers and yells for you. I know what it is like to feel the pressure of everyone on your shoulders, and I know what it is like to choke under the pressure. I know what it means to be an athlete, a true player, and that is why I play. I am an athlete. A champion. A true player..."

Are you?

CHAPTER 4

CREATING A PERSONAL HIGHLIGHT REEL IN YOUR HEAD

There's an anonymous quote that goes, "It's not who you are that holds you back, it's who you think you're not." Of course, no one's suggesting you go the route of narcissism, but there are overwhelming psychological and performance benefits that occur when you cast yourself as the star of your own highlight reel. We're not talking about a literal, video-screened version of events, but rather a developing "film" you imagine of yourself, seeing yourself in your head clearly – and most importantly, enjoyably. Now is the opportune time to be the writer, director, producer, and actor in the personal highlight reel of your mind.

From the Projects to the Pros (Seeing It Before It Happens)

Throughout my high school, college, and NFL careers, I was fortunate enough to have multiple excellent head coaches and assistant coaches. Coach Andy Hinson was my coach at Camden High School, and he had a great impact on my life. He was a father figure for me. He knew I had the athletic ability to earn a scholarship in either basketball or football. When making the decision, he had me visualize putting a reel in my head, so to speak, to figure out which sport would be to my advantage. At that particular time, I was about 6'7" and weighed about 190 pounds. He helped me to reason in my mind how many basketball players are that height compared to football players. Where would be my advantage? I wanted to play in a Big 10 school, and some of the schools I visited were the University of Michigan, the University of Minnesota, and Michigan State. I was sold on Michigan State, but again, Coach Hinson had me visualize where the best opportunity for me to be able to play and make a name for myself. With that reasoning, I eventually went to the University of Kentucky because they were rebuilding and were looking to build a championship team. They were known for their basketball program, and in this situation, I would have the opportunity if I played well in football. I could make my own name.

The one person who helped me understand the importance of visualization, not just in the game, but in every aspect of my life, was Marv Levy, my first NFL coach who drafted me in 1978. He is in the Pro Football Hall of Fame and went to the Super Bowl four years in a row. Three things that stand out to me even to this day were his constant sermons on the value of visualization, playing with tenacity, and preparation. Paying attention to the details of the game plan involved preparation (watching films, practicing plays and techniques, strength and conditioning, nutrition, proper sleep, and so on).

One of things I have come to appreciate about visualization is that in your mind, ideally, everything you visualize, you do. One example is playing a perfect game. With regard to that, I am still working on that perfect game. That being said, that's where it comes into play when something goes wrong, individually or as a team, you are able to visualize what went wrong on that particular play or series of plays and correct it in your mind. The whole objective is so that it won't happen again, but as I mentioned before, I am still visualizing.

Highlighted Power

University of Michigan head basketball coach John Beilein, like most coaches and sports psychologists, recognizes the power of highlight reels. "Throughout the NCAA Tournament," Beilein said, "it is easy for players to see themselves on ESPN and highlight reels and begin to think about how good they are. However, while some teams are relishing their success, others are in the gym and film room looking for ways to get better."

Former New York Giants coach Tom Coughlin noted that he allows music to be mixed into the highlight reels that he uses to motivate his players.

Highlight reels are typically thought of as those special moments on the sports news screen, but highlight reels don't always have to be taped events. The best viewing can occur right in your own head. To make it even better, that highlight reel does not have to be based on facts as they are now, but rather on your vision for the future. So how does that come about, and why does this reel – which can occur in various proportions of reality or fantasy – mean so much?

How you see yourself affects everything else that you do in your life. This is so evident today with personal exposure on social media. Every post, picture share, like, and comment takes on the quality of a personal highlight reel that is open to the world, and that means you need to show the world your best "you." How do you do that? By asking yourself, "What do I want playing on my highlights reel? What do I want my story to be?"

New Reels in New Ways

Highlights that have been video recorded are long-proven tools coaches use to create powerful teachable moments. They're used to enforce objectives and for motivation. Videos are often used to visually reinforce proper techniques and as a visual reminder of goals and objectives, which in turn serves as motivation. Digital video images of an athlete performing well can be edited to create fantasy match-ups of local athletes playing along with the greats of the game, to aspire the at-home athlete to be like the famous sports hero, or even to conquer the established star athlete.

New technology includes an app that is touted to have incredible power and precision used for tagging video. Coaches find tagging useful as the action happens live. But the great thing is, when it comes to making your "personal highlight reel," you can do the same thing that real coaches use in order to motivate their players, no app necessary. You just use your imagination to create your own motivational imagery through the lens of your mind's eye.

The Highlight Reels that are Projected

Personal highlight reels aren't like a static photo finish. They're a dynamic embellishment of the individual's wishes, dreams, and hopes all layered onto an experience or all-encompassing concept. Don't fall into a trap of feeling lessened by learning about someone else's highlight reel. Avoid getting lost comparing someone else's reel to what you know yours to be from your own personal place of behind-the-scenes reflection. Chances are you could very well be comparing your weakest moment to other people's strongest. Keep your own highlight reel playing, and keep it in focus.

You on ESPN

If you haven't seen this highlight reel in your head yet, it is never too late to start. Turn on your internal personal highlight reel and visualize yourself in the highlights of yesterday's fabulous performance. The personal highlight reel we're talking about is also called high-level visualization. You use your skills of visualizing to create your reel. You clearly see yourself doing a certain play, a certain task that lives up to your ultimate desires and dreams. Sports psychologists agree that a minute of visualization is worth seven minutes of practice.

A Vision for Your Own Eyes in Your Head

If you've never tried visualizing before, here are some tips on how to go about it.

1. Your inner eye is your camera as you imagine your scene.

2. Pay attention to your senses – sight, hearing, smell, taste, and touch – to experience all the details.

3. Visualize the whole scene, from warm-up to the end, and note your feelings and thoughts at different points throughout. Make sure to put your focus on how you want to feel at these points.

4. Be aware of the results you wish for.

5. Note how you feel when you are doing your best, when you have done your best, and when you see yourself successful and winning.

6. If something goes wrong, replay your scene and fix it.

7. You can watch your visualization at whatever speed you wish – slowing down or speeding up at any time.

8. Allow yourself to experience elated emotions and give yourself credit for your successes.

9. Finalize your visualization with seeing yourself performing exactly the way you want to (including warm-up), your event, results, and handling pressures and competition. In your personal highlights, you are the most prepared and most successful athlete there ever was.

10. Repeat your visualization many times so your head and body are trained to be stronger each time.

Start Here... Your Great Performance

Sport psychologists agree that if you have a strong belief in, and can imagine what your ability to perform well looks like, your chances are the best for actually doing so, and for continually improving your physical performances. What is in your head helps you with personal judgments, self-coaching, calmness, confidence, focusing on necessities, and improving your maximum performance and potential – even beyond what you envision in your mind.

Creating your personal highlight reel in your head that you can use daily, even before falling asleep, before training or workouts, or competitions, is valuable to your success and your greatness. So first of all, determine what you want to accomplish and what it will take for you to achieve it. Avoid thinking of the obstacles that might be in your way, but focus instead on you and your path to success. Avoid thinking about what you don't want to do, and think instead about what you do want to do. Think only about what you want to happen. This method, often called a "performance statement," helps you to avoid self-doubt, negativity, and head chatter – which in turn gets you to your best performance during your tasks.

To create your performance statement, here are two tips:

1. Think about a huge, major competition, real or imaginary. Now, immediately before it begins, your coach tells you to focus on two things for your success. What are those things?

2. Still imagining that major competition, put yourself in the place of coach as well as the athlete. Again, think of the two things that the coach would name and what you will think in response. This will help you to know your own positive thinking and scripting ahead of time so you will do it naturally, without reverting to negative thinking and mental clutter that will slow you down.

That Compelling Reason

Sport psychotherapists have long advocated using the personal internal highlights reel method when working with individuals on increasing self-awareness, identifying best mental zones, and developing tools to regulate themselves to reach those zones. The personal highlights reel is a central part of a five-prong plan for a mental workout. Coaches often describe this as a mental workout. It's the SportsCenter you carry around with you at all times.

They suggest to first look for and find that compelling emotional reason to pursue your goals, such as "to feel strong and powerful in my body." Vague reasons are not helpful or effective. With something specific in mind, the individual is then encouraged to make a personal highlight reel of times in his or her life when he or she felt this way, and it's fine to improve or expand it. Think of other images that connect with this passion for the sport. This might include best performances, admirable athletes, and a vision of the self as powerful and fast and strong. The athlete is encouraged to imagine these highlights as a reel using all the senses – what you hear, how your body feels, and what you're thinking and feeling. Therapists suggest running the reel through your head two or three times in succession, once or twice a day.

Just a 5-Minute Plan

The Daily 5-Minute Plan, supported in notable books, lectures, and counseling programs begins with a 15-second centering breath.

Step 1 is the centering breath, which is important for controlling heart rate, arousal state, and the ability to think. The breathing is a normal breath. Breathe in for six seconds, hold it there for two, and then breathe out for seven.

Step 2 is a performance or identity statement in which you state to yourself what your own focus is and your declaration about what you believe it takes to be successful – essentially who you are and what you want to achieve.

Step 3 is the personal highlight reel. This is your own SportsCenter show for your head. You watch yourself living your dreams to the max and playing at your peak. To make your best personal highlight reel, first spend a few minutes visualizing what success looks like to you – famous people, admirable people, yourself. Then you're ready to make your mind's reel, which is made up of three 60-second parts.

The first part is a replay of your past successes, remembering at least three things you recently did well. In the second part, you imagine success in an upcoming day by focusing on three things you *will* do well, what you need to do to be great. Think about just how you want to feel – before, during, and after that event – and consider your focus, how you want to manage pressure, and how you want to achieve your desired success. Use as much detail as possible. In the third part, you "see" yourself playing that successful game. See it – visualize yourself feeling confident, focused, and performing top notch. See yourself be successful.

Step 4 is a repeat of your performance or identity statement, which helps solidify your self-image and remind yourself of your best strength and your ability to accomplish great things. Whatever you tell yourself is correct! Coaches and psychologists alike counsel that if you tell yourself you can and will accomplish your dreams, you boost the likelihood of succeeding. Sports psychologists find this a proven tool for self-confidence, which is also a dependable, essential, and helpful factor to improved performance.

Step 5 finishes with another centering 15-second deep breath.

From Video Reel in Your Head to Your Complete Experience

With practice, your highlights reel can become more than just a reel in your mind. You can authentically experience what you are imagining, even with sounds and smells, as long as you get into the realistic nitty gritty of the whole – how you felt, the reactions of your family on the sidelines, and the expressions and reactions of the team or coaches. Maybe it's one of your first wins.

The Real Reel

Of course, actual recorded highlight reels have a purpose too, and with video technology so accessible these days, you don't have to be a pro with ESPN clips to make a useful one. It's every person's human experience to have ups and downs, but not every person deals with those ups and downs effectively. Relish the ups. They are a vital part of your highlight reel.

One reputable leadership coach and iron man triathlon racer described her own highlight reel that has helped her through five years of iron man racing ups and downs. Her reel reflected on her first iron man triathlon at age 53, which she admitted was painful, but a highlight of her life nevertheless. Crossing the finish line, she realized she was hooked on that feeling of having given everything she had to a goal, pushing herself beyond what she ever thought possible, and accomplishing it. Realizing it. And reviewing her highlight reel with this finish line experience in there gets her through new goals, disappointments, and setbacks – all because her highlight reel keeps on inspiring her with energy, confidence, and self-knowledge.

Highlights Never Forgotten

Exciting sports news not only leads to exciting highlight reels for contemporary sportscasts, but highlights last in the memories of both participants and fans throughout their lives. They serve as a constant motivator for reaching the best in everything. One aging sports enthusiast published a glowing tribute to memorable sports highlights. He recalled, "A half-dozen 60-somethings, who at that moment probably couldn't have located their car keys, began identifying each team member, detailing the position he played, the abilities he possessed or lacked, the future he would lead. Soon, our athletic autopsy had achieved such microscopic focus that we were recalling intramural games from a half-century ago."

He contemplated the reasons why the huge variety of stored memories was so indelible and vivid over the years. He concluded with the reiteration of the concept that sports psychologists and athletic coaches and directors offer about the impact of highlights reels: "Those memories of having starred – even having just played or watched – help define many of us. We attend because we hope we come away with a moment we can recount forever. They instantly become significant parts of our personal narratives."

And finally, he concluded with reasons that sports psychologists and athletic leaders also offer about the value of highlight reels, and especially personal highlights reels: "Those memories might be serving a necessary psychological function, crowding out the unease, the angst, and the occasional unpleasantness."

Breaking Records

Maybe you want to be a record breaker, so why not go the distance with your personal highlight reel? Imagine yourself as Denver Broncos kicker Matt Prater setting a new NFL record with a 64-yard field goal. Or envision the record-breaking feat of your own dreams. Make your personal highlight reel an eternal fountain of the wins you want.

———∼∼∼———

SECTION 11

YOU GOTTA BELIEVE

"To believe in yourself and to follow your dreams... this is success!"

                                                    —Sasha Azevedo

"Ask me, I'll play. Ask me, I'll shoot. Ask me, I'll pass. It's not what you ask. It's what I ask of myself."

                                                    —LeBron James

"I am the greatest; I said that even before I knew I was."

                                                    —Muhammad Ali

"In my mind, I'm always the best. If I walk out on the court and I think the next person is better, I've already lost."

                                                    —Venus Williams

"You owe it to yourself to be the best you can possibly be in baseball and in life."

                                                    —Pete Rose

"Good, better, best. Never let it rest. Until your good is better and your better is best."

                                                    —Tim Duncan, NBA MVP

CHAPTER 5

SETTING GOALS, ON AND OFF THE FIELD

Goals are the objects of many sports - whether we're talking about individual points scored or the desire to win the game. Athletes and spectators are aware of the goals — the outcomes they want to see in the sports they follow. But before an athlete walks out onto the playing field, there's another goal to consider. It's actually all about the steps, about planning where to go and keeping track of the journey. All the steps to get out there on the field add up and count as goals in and of themselves. Once you're on that field, then, more "points" get added as necessary. It's a process: planning, tracking, and scoring goals, on and off the field. Sports psychology supports the fact that this process of establishing goals is the way to assure optimal success.

From the Projects to the Pros (Each Stepping Stone Along The Way)

As an athlete, speaking for myself, you have to have goals in order to succeed. This is Life 101. My objective coming from Camden, New Jersey was leaving the projects by using my athletic abilities. But first things first: I had to get the grades and graduate or my initial goal would never have been possible. Everything started clicking in high school that if I wanted to get out of Camden, I had to first get good grades or I would not be able to get a scholarship for my athletic ability. In high school, besides my coaches and counselors, the single most positive influence was my principal, Mrs. Riletta Cream. She was married to Jersey Joe Walcott. Jersey Joe was an American professional boxer who held the world heavyweight title from 1951-1952, and broke the record for the oldest man to win the title at the age of 37, a record that was eventually broken by George Foreman. Jersey Joe is a legend from Camden, New Jersey.

Looking back, I had an all-pro support team, people such as Mr. Jenkins, Mr. McFadden, Coach Hinson, Coach Turner, Mr. Walter, and all the assistant coaches for basketball, football, and track. (I apologize for not being able to name everyone.) Also, my teammates were a huge support because we pushed each other. We all had the same goal to use our athletic ability to make something out of life for our families.

Give Yourself the Reasons

Of course, you have your own compelling reasons for why you're into your given sport. You know how you'd like to perform and what you want to achieve. Ideally, your reasons for wanting those goals are your own – for yourself and not anyone else, not to please pals, parents, other family members, or doctors. And remember, to give you an additional boost and compel you even further in the positive direction, you've got your personal highlight reel in your head that we talked about in the last chapter.

This chapter is about goals. Research shows a self-perpetuating goal cycle: athletes and sports enthusiasts with goals that bring them happiness (ones they are passionate about) are motivated to reach them, and then they set additional goals that bring more happiness. It's an ongoing system.

Think about the important aspects of your life and how your goals get interwoven to fit in. Think about the person you see yourself becoming or wish to become. Ask yourself: what are the three most important things in your life, and will your goals and actions reflect your own priorities?

What Do Goals Accomplish for Athletes?

Goals motivate players to use and develop existing talents and abilities. Goals bring necessary knowledge for specific tasks into the athlete's awareness. Goals can inspire an athlete to search for new knowledge, especially when investigating new and/or complex tasks.

Motivational Movement – Two Types, One Goal

So you have your goals, but what is it that moves you forward so you can pursue and reach those goals? Researchers have discovered that athletes exhibit either a *fixed* mindset or a *growth* mindset regarding skills and endurance.

With autonomous motives that originate from a growth mindset, an athlete might say, "I enjoy trying to achieve my goal. My goal is important and will improve my performance." With controlling motives that come from a fixed mindset, an athlete might say, "If I didn't pursue my goals, I sure would feel guilty" or something like, "Both my coach and my family expect me to go for my goals."

A growth mindset is associated with autonomous motives such as enjoyment, personal importance, and love of the sport. Athletes who have growth mindsets and attitudes were found to be empowered by believing in themselves. They have faith that they can be successful and accomplish anything they set out to do. Research has determined that an athlete with a growth mindset is able to reach higher levels of performance. However, when athletes have a fixed idea about their levels of skill or endurance, they set their goals at lower levels to avoid any embarrassment they might have to endure in front of other people.

To further their research in these areas, sports psychologists conducted experiments in which athletes on stationary bikes underwent performance tests. The athletes had already established goals regarding their speed and distance. However, the cycles were manipulated to give false readings in order to see how the test subject athletes would respond in situations of stress and discouragement. Their speeds and distance were monitored in front of them for continuous feedback. The researchers found that those athletes with a growth mindset put in more effort. They worked longer and harder than those with a fixed attitude to reach the goals initially set.

Even the Best Can Do Better

Skills are the easiest way to visually measure an athlete's abilities and potential for success. And no matter what skill is observed, everyone knows there's always room for improvement.

Research on expert and high-level performances of athletes in soccer, netball, basketball, field hockey, and triathlons showed positive skill level improvement in highly structured activities when the athletes aimed to improve. The researchers believe these positive results are due to passion as a motivational force that leads a player to keep up with demanding practice activities that can be dull, repetitive, and not always enjoyable.

Coaches of winning athletes describe them as participants who achieve continuing skill development. For example, they point to Michael Jordan, who is reported to have typically stayed an extra 45 minutes to work on specific skills such as a fade-away jump shot, even after regular team practice finished.

In his book *Slaying the Dragon,* sprinter Michael Johnson reflects on effective goal setting, which helped him win Olympic gold medals. His book reveals how significant improvements in performance can be achieved by effective goal setting. Johnson's recommendations on goal setting are supported by research in sports and exercise that has long shown how goal setting can lead to enhanced performance. Recent statistics report that 78% of those studied exhibited performance enhancement with moderate to strong results based on goal setting.

The Purpose of Goals

When describing success in all fields – from top-level athletes to business people – goal setting is the key to the road map of success. The following are some reasons that researchers and sports leaders agreed upon:

- Setting goals gives you long-term vision and short-term motivation.

- Goals get you focused on your acquisition of knowledge.

- Goals help you organize your time and your resources so you can make the most of your life.

- By setting sharp, clearly defined goals, you can measure and take pride in the achievement of those goals, and you'll see progress in what might previously have seemed like a long, pointless grind.

- You will also raise your self-confidence as you recognize your own ability and competence in achieving the goals that you've set.

- Goal setting requires communication, commitment, buy-in, and negotiation by everyone involved.

Setting Goals the SMART Way

Sports psychologists and goals counselors advise athletes to use the Be-SMART plan for setting goals. Setting goals should follow this simple rule: Be-SMART.

SMART stands for:

S - Specific (or Significant).

M - Measurable (or Meaningful).

A - Attainable (or Action-Oriented).

R - Relevant (or Rewarding).

T - Time-bound (or Trackable).

Psychologists suggest considering the following when planning your goals:

1. Be specific. What skill or situation do you want to work on?

2. Create a confident mindset. Talk to yourself and tell yourself that you will do what you plan, and you will perform these activities with excellence.

3. Use mental imagery to envision your actions – performing the skill or play just as you'd like to see it happen in real life.

4. Create some space. As you plan your schedules for working toward your goals, make sure you also allow time to focus, recharge, and renewal.

5. Make decisive plans. Research has shown that momentum builds with decisive action, while lack of clarity and confusion gets in the way of momentum.

6. Avoid being a perfectionist. Rather than focusing on being perfect, focus on being effective. Develop methods to make it right and make it work. Think of practice as a process of continuing improvement.

7. Find your flow in your actions. Flow adds to your enjoyment and power and leads to full engagement. Flow can occur when your goals are clear, when you have good feedback, when you are challenged by what you are working on, and when you have confidence in yourself. When your goals are clear and you have feedback for each goal as you work on it, you are on the right track.

8. Know what your "one thing" is and your compelling "why." These specifics will inspire you through thick and thin.

9. See your goals in your mind's eye. Just like with actions (number 3), when you can visualize something it is easier to achieve it.

10. Dream big. Set extreme goals as well as intermediary ones.

11. Use your past, present, or future as motivation for setting your goals. For example, use your victories from the past, your present learning experiences, and your future dreams.

12. Transform any "have to" into a "choose to." Choice is a powerful motivator.

13. Pursue your goals with compelling passion.

Achievement Goals

Achievement is traditionally associated with those standardized tests you took in school, but major researchers of high-performance sports have also described three standards of achievement goals that apply in the school of life:

- Mastery goals, which are how competence is developed in the tasks of training for the sport

- Performance approach goals, which are what the athlete wants and works to achieve in personal competence in relation to others

- Performance avoidance goals, which are the incompetence or weaknesses that the athlete wants to avoid in relation to others, and works on to overcome

What the Coaches Say

Coaches also describe goals in their own terms with tips for using them with success.

Results Goals

According to coaches of champions, these are goals to set and use before and after a game or a practice session. Here's the rundown on results goals:

- Make these goals measurable.

- Choose about three goals.

- Keep a daily log for your results goals. It might take you all of four minutes to write down what you did well in your practice.

- Also write down one thing you would like to improve in your next practice.

- Write down one thing you can do differently that can make that improvement happen.

- Write down what you might have to sacrifice in order to accomplish this goal.

- Write down what strengths you have that you can use to make these improvements.

- Take one more minute to review this entry, which will add to your motivation.

Process Goals

These are the goals you set for yourself for your practice. These goals are what you want to work on in order to reach your successful results goals. Process goals can include mental training goals. Mental training will be covered in more detail in a later chapter.

Ultimate Goal

This is the long run goal – the goal of your career. This is the goal of what you ultimately want to accomplish and how you will get to that.

Setting them High

When people talk about achievement, whether scaling a mountain or scoring on an exam, we use words related to getting to the top, the peak, and the heights, and it is the same with setting goals. Aim high!

Sport psychologists agree that athletic success is best achieved through setting high but realistic goals, as well as through training and playing hard.

The Ohio Center for Sport Psychology runs such a program. The center prioritizes the success of serious athletes, and this is reflected in their list of top three procedures. Setting high, realistic goals follows maintaining a positive attitude and adhering to a high level of self-motivation.

At the Ohio Center, both long-term and short-term goals are measurable and time-oriented. The setting of goals allows for tracking current performance levels, as well as for developing specific and detailed plans for reaching each goal. In addition to the athlete's higher level of goal commitment is the athlete's participation in daily tasks and the necessary demands of training, which are all essential components of the center's goal-setting program.

Set Them High or Low?

Research has shown that higher levels of performance on tasks and more successes result from setting specific higher goals than from easy or vague goals. Vague or abstract goals include goals such as "to do one's best." The loftier and more specific the goal, the better.

Researchers explain that high goals motivate an athlete with self-satisfaction in his or her performance. Hard goals require the athlete to reach for and attain more, and when achieved, result in greater satisfaction than easy goals. Hard or high goals also lead to higher levels of persistence and effort.

Those More Challenging Goals

Both psychological research and the feedback from sports coaches support the notion that much of the success experienced by motivated athletes comes from setting challenging goals and their abilities to manage the process of achieving those goals. The levels of involvement and commitment to activities were described by one coach as indicating which athletes would be successful at achieving high-level performance goals.

This coach described a method he uses with his players, and what outcomes he might expect to see. He asks the athletes to perform a drill, demonstrating the skill first, then discussing the purpose of the drill. He asks for questions, demonstrates a second time for reinforcement, and then steps away for the players to try it out. This coach then went on to describe how one player performs the activity correctly. Another player performs it correctly as well, but adds an element of speed to test his ability and skill level when he moves faster. A third player performs correctly, and also performs the activity at speed and exhibits some practical thinking by continuing the activity while exhibiting another skill. The coach explained that the first player performed correctly as needed, but the second and third players challenged themselves to perform at a higher level than just the minimum. They set a more challenging goal right then and there, and they worked to achieve it.

How to Apply Challenges to Your Goals

One coach suggested several tips in the form of questions to consider when planning out your goals. He explains that questions are the best way to increase options, get a foothold into leverage, challenge your own present views, and enable the possibilities of switching to more empowering goals and mindsets.

Ask yourself the following:

1. What's a better way to perform this task?

2. How can I enjoy performing this particular skill or act?

3. What would _____ (the name of a champion in this particular sport) do?

4. If I were my coach, what would I tell myself?

5. At the top of your game, when you reach your best shot, what is your new personal best?

"Not Every Four Years, Every Day"

This is what a sign says on a door at the U.S. Olympic Training Center. It reminds athletes in high-performance sports that their goals of excellence come from their little daily successes.

The Secret of Getting to Your Goals

Coaches and sports psychologists alike, as well as the most successful athletes, emphasize hard work, and they acknowledge that it may often seem boring. One coach describes it as, "shake it off and step up, don't do your best, you have to do whatever it takes." He points out that even with less than natural talent, an athlete doing all the little extras – the uncomfortable things, looking always for ways to become smarter, stronger, faster, and better conditioned – is the work of getting to every goal. Seeing this work as opportunities, challenges, and stepping-stones makes it anything but boring.

He agrees that there are athletes who complain about practicing hard. He says that those who think there is nothing to be gained by pushing themselves, or who practice without being serious, are fooling themselves when it comes to preparation. And their bad habits will sooner or later catch up with them.

Another coach describes getting comfortable with being uncomfortable as the only method of getting to your goals. It's the formula for success. He's seen it happen over and over: the more an athlete can challenge his or her comfort and refuse to be satisfied with the status quo, the faster his or her development, progress, and accomplishment.

Confidence, Commitment, and Champions

Psychology research has long discussed the principle of cognitive dissonance, and this principle applies to the success of athletes on their path to realizing their goals. The more you are committed to your own beliefs and affirm that you are indeed on the right path, the less likely it is that you'll doubt yourself or judge yourself as wrong even when faced with alleged evidence to the contrary.

Everyone goes through rough patches. Those hard times along the path of working toward goals can make it seem like the wrong path. But research shows how commitment and belief keep successful people going and not wavering or buckling. Commitment is required for staying the course and not giving up.

Coaches in all sports agree that what separates top performers from everyone else is that they stick with their goals, no matter how they feel. In other words, they don't allow their fleeting emotions to determine their actions. Their enduring passion and love for their sport keep them dedicated to the process. These athletes work when work isn't easy, and they work when it's boring or when they honestly don't feel like being there at that time.

Learning Goals vs. Performance Goals

Having a goal that focuses on attaining knowledge, task mastery, and skills needed to reach a goal was found to lead to better performance than goals that are too specific and focused on performance outcomes. Researchers believe that the learning goal mindset helps the planning, monitoring, and evaluating of progress toward reaching goals.

Related studies found that those with a learning goal chose tasks where they could learn the skills and attain the knowledge for their goal, while those with performance goal orientation would avoid tasks where they could be embarrassed or unfavorably judged due to mistakes they could make. Therefore, they chose easier tasks in order to look good to others.

Other researchers also determined performance goal orientation to be associated with goal-avoidance motivation, lower goal levels, and lower performance.

Short-Term Goals and Long-Term Dream Goals

Research has shown that long-term or "dream" goals alone will not lead to better performances, but are valuable for directing efforts. Long-term goals can be six months to several years away. However, it is the short-term and intermediate goals that lead to success. Intermediate goals mark progress along your path and indicate where you want to be at certain intervals, generally during three to five months. Short-term are daily goals and are most important in providing focus for daily training. Focusing on one small step at a time develops confidence that allows you to move on to more challenging tasks and goals.

But what if the goal is not feasible?

Of course, it is still important for athletes to be able to recognize when a course of action really does need to be changed, if the methods are not working toward achieving the specific goal.

Keeping it Real

Recent research from the Sports Psychology Lab at the Universities of Birmingham and Southampton explains the success of athletes who can effectively manage their goals, such as Andy Murray. Following a back injury, Murray dropped out of the French Open so he could recuperate, which then allowed him to play at Wimbledon. The research revealed that if athletes recognized early enough that a goal was unattainable and switched their goals to new ones that lead up to their main objectives, they would still most likely be successful in attaining those goals.

The study looked at the motivation of athletes who are likely to be able to make this kind of a goal switch. The researchers found that athletes motivated by enjoyment or the personal importance of their goals were able to push themselves to work harder, longer, and achieve successes in increasingly difficult goals, as opposed to those motivated by other pressures or guilty feelings. These athletes with autonomous motives also experienced an increased sense of well-being from achieving their goals.

However, the researchers also found that self-motivated athletes did find it more difficult to stop working toward their initial goal, and continued persistence could cause psychological distress. But again, the distress was avoided when the highly motivated athletes recognized early enough when a goal was impossible, and then they were able to easily disengage from that one and start with challenging new goals along with their original overall objectives. These athletes were shown to be most successful in achieving their major goal.

On the other side, athletes with controlled or fixed motives don't persist if a goal becomes more difficult. They feel goals are less important, and they're less confident in their skills and abilities to achieve their goal.

The researchers summed up that coaches and sports psychologists should be aware of the motivation behind the goals of athletes in order to best help them be adaptive and successful in reaching their goals. They suggested athletes use a daily training diary to measure the performances of their short-term and intermediate goals. When they are using data instead of emotions, better decisions can be made concerning the best path – whether to continue with or switch interim goals.

Coaches can also encourage athletes to set flexible, autonomous goals and help with implementing action plans.

Review, Rundown, and Recap

Goal setting works by providing direction for efforts, focusing in for attention, promoting persistence, and increasing confidence in achieving intermediate goals.

To recap, here are the highlights and tips that sports psychologists and coaches agree upon when it comes to goal setting:

1. Decide what you want. Have your vision, your dream, and make sure it is personal.

2. Commit to your goals. Your goals have to be worth going for.

3. Believe that you can attain your goals. They should not be too easy or unrealistic.

4. Set objective goals – ones that are measurable and able to be evaluated, rather than vague, such as "to do my best."

5. Focus on one step at a time. Focus on one dream goal, two or three intermediate goals, and two short-term goals at a time.

6. Consider any potential barriers to your goals and plan around them.

Have three types of goals:

1. Outcome goals that focus on objective results. These provide motivation.

2. Performance goals that are flexible and work with your own comparison of previous performances. Athletes can directly control performance goals, thus allowing them to better improve capabilities. These are often short-term goals.

3. Process goals, which deal with the skills, actions, and techniques you need to attain your success.

Results goals can't be controlled and can increase negative stress and pressure, so it's best to focus on the three goal types listed above.

Remember that many researchers recommend the SMART approach to goal setting. Goals should be specific, measurable, accepted as worthwhile, realistic and attainable, recorded, and time-specific.

The best outcomes result from a combination of the various goal strategies described in this chapter.

CHAPTER 6

THE THREE CS: CONFIDENCE, COURAGE, AND COMMITMENT

How do you spell success? In the world of athletic success, there are actually three Cs that you'll need to remember in order to get that word right: confidence, courage, and commitment.

These three Cs pertain to thoughts that anyone can have through the power of choice, which by the way, is another awesome C-word. Choose to think in ways that help you deliver your best.

From the Projects to the Pros (Putting the Three Cs Into Action)

In order to be a positive influence on the team, you have to have confidence in your abilities to contribute to the ultimate goal for the team. Speaking on the term "positive," confidence really goes back to preparation and doing your homework. For me, confidence means the psychological and physical side of things, which works hand in hand with one another. For example, when playing in the NFL, one of the many things that enhanced my confidence was something that most people at that time would never thought about: nutrition. Today, we know that nutrition plays a vital role in an athlete's performance, but back when I played, it was not the norm. Some people called me "the fruit and nut man." My healthy dietary choices gave me confidence, because making an informed decision about what I was eating gave me the edge I needed as a player. For example: the night before a game, I had a different routine than most players. I ate food that was easily digestible and nutritious. Then on game day, my pre-game meal was even more modified, and I was also drinking plenty of water. In my visualization, I could see my opponent eating a big greasy steak with eggs and potatoes along with a big glass of milk. Research shows that eating certain types of food takes more energy to digest, especially when competing on a physical level.

As you can see, this was a confidence-builder for me that took courage to be different. But I was committed to using what I learned to my advantage.

Confidence

Some coaches preach the differences of the right kind of thinking versus the wrong kind of thinking. Negative and destructive thoughts are self-defeating, can hurt practice and performances, and can even destroy the enjoyment of your sport. Positive thoughts, however, are those focused, enhancing thoughts that build your enjoyment and lead to increased levels of success.

Research studies agree that the right thoughts begin with confidence – trusting yourself to deliver your best.

Champions glow with confidence. It's not a secret ingredient that only a select few possess, but rather a way of thinking that's available for anyone to develop. The three Cs form a triangle with confidence at its base. Many studies point out that courage and commitment are built upon confidence.

Coaches and sports psychologists describe confidence as the quality that motivates an athlete and allows them to accept and accomplish what might otherwise seem too difficult or impossible. Confidence keeps an athlete working hard even though there are setbacks and failures, no matter what obstacles show up on the path.

Confidence is like a cousin to positive mental thinking. It's what gives athletes and their teams the courage to focus on strengths in the face of strong opponents and challenges. Confidence makes it obvious that athletes are enjoying their sport because they feel great about the game and about themselves. They feel – they *know* – that anything can be accomplished. The fear of losing ceases.

Your confidence shows in performances that exceed expectations because of how you play to your full potential. The sky's the limit, as the saying goes.

Confidence Busters

So how does an athlete develop or gain confidence? One way is by recognizing and getting rid of what winning coaches refer to as "confidence busters." Confidence busters are natural feelings of doubt that everyone experiences at some point. They include questioning one's abilities, feeling overwhelmed, being easily psyched out, lacking zip and energy, being off in timing, feeling weak and vulnerable, and being easily distracted by worries. Confidence busters are those moments when there's a battle going on in your head, one voice that's saying, "be confident," while the other says, "no chance, loser." Confidence busters may even make you question whether you should still be playing your sport.

Step Up to Confidence

Sports confidence coaches recommend 10 steps to help keep confidence up front and in top form.

1. Do your physical training solidly by doing what is possible in your power, doing what is expected, and then do a little more each time. When you know you've done the work, you know you have the right to feel confident. You can even feel confident that you've trained longer and harder than others who are tough competitors.

2. Remind yourself all the time that you are putting in great training and that you're doing all you can to prepare yourself. When you are effective and productive in practice and training, you cannot help

but see your physical skills increase. As you improve, your confidence increases because of your ability to perform at a higher level and your sense of continued improvement. Reminding yourself can eliminate nervousness and pressure that clouds your clear focus at game time. You will have the confidence in knowing you've done everything possible in training, and so you're ready when the whistle blows.

3. Stay focused on yourself instead of comparing yourself to others, which is unfair and draining to confidence. Many coaches have affirmed that in any sport or game, it is not necessarily the best athlete or team that shows up as champion (stronger, faster, high jumping etc.). but the athlete or team with confidence.

4. Focus on what you can control and lock onto it. There will always be things beyond your control that can make you tighten up and test your confidence, such as physical conditions on the field, memories of the past, and various fleeting ideas or other people's words about the outcomes. Don't sabotage your confidence by drifting away from what you can control.

5. Confidence is described by coaches and sports psychologists as the bright side of looking at a challenge. Negative thinking zaps confidence. Like the message in the Broadway hit *Wicked*, things depend on how you look at them. There can be unfortunate truths, such as challenging weather, but take the positive, confident note and focus on how it will affect your opponents more than you.

6. Reward your daily victories, which are all the little things you do right. Don't disregard or take them for granted – catch yourself doing something a little better, a little stronger, farther, faster, or higher, and then record it! When you habitually add up your small victories and write them down, you will have a daily confidence builder that increases automatically.

7. Forgive yourself for setbacks, losses, and mistakes. Don't dwell on them, but forgive yourself for what's normal. Get over it and move on.

8. Know your own personal confidence builders. What works best for some may not be tops for others, but they usually include pep talks, self-talk, surrounding yourself with supportive people who believe in you, taking care of your daily diet and health, and having the best possible proper equipment and training opportunities with great coaches.

9. Make a sports feedback journal to check on your thinking processes right after practice or competitions. Record your thoughts about your performance to see if you have any lapses in confidence or sabotaging, doubtful, fearful feelings. If you do, reform each one into a positive affirmation and record it and practice it.

10. Prepare additional powerful affirmations to make them an automatic part of your self-talk. For example, "I can do this, I play well under pressure. I am fast. I am a strong hitter. When the game is on the line, I love taking the shot." Use "I am, I will, I have," rather than "I want" or "I hope".

Confidence, Performance, and Success

Studies have shown supporting evidence that confidence is directly related to performance. Thus, it's one of the most important tools for an athlete's success. Famed golfer Jack Nicklaus said, "Confidence is the most important single factor in this game, and no matter how great your natural talent, there is only one way to obtain and sustain it: work."

Sports psychologist Dr. Kate Hays has much to share about confidence stemming from her work with Olympic and world-class athletes. "The most consistent finding in sport psychology research," Hays said, "is the direct correlation between high levels of sport confidence and success in sports performances."

Dr. Hays studied where confidence comes from. Her research revealed that basing confidence on winning can result in a confidence blow when winning does not occur. She continued to explain that athletes need to develop confidence from not one, but several sources – the strongest coming from a focus on the self and one's own processes and goals that are obtained through training, preparation, and goal setting. It's less productive to worry about uncontrollable events and outcomes. Therefore, Dr. Hays explained, goals should be process- and performance-based, since the outcome goal of winning "won't help them run the race." Dr. Hays described results showing that athletes do struggle with confidence, especially after a poor performance, injury, or from personal put-downs. This sports psychology research shows that confidence born from right thinking is the key to distinguishing successful and unsuccessful sports performances.

No Doubt About It… or Maybe Just a Little

On the other hand, Dr. Deborah Feltz of the Department of Kinesiology at Michigan State reported that some doubts can be a good motivation in training, and they can help build confidence and make goals attainable. But at the point of competition, there should not be any doubts about succeeding in your goals.

Feeling Confident

Some sports researchers describe confidence as thinking, others as feeling. Regardless, both are involved, and research illustrates this truth. Dr. Alan Goldberg explained that confidence is something to feel. In running, for example, thinking about stride or an arm position slows you down and puts you in the wrong part of your brain for top performance, whereas feeling your running – letting your shoulder loosen, feeling your fists unclenched – will "put you in the zone." Dr. Goldberg also notes that there's a fine line between confidence and arrogance.

Venus Williams once said, "Some people say I have attitude, maybe I do… but I think you have to. You have to believe in yourself when no one else does – that makes you a winner right there."

The Confidence Challenge

Coaches and sports psychologists agree that the biggest challenge to confidence is how to respond when things aren't going your way. The best athletes can maintain their confidence when they are not winning, when they're not at the top of their game, when conditions aren't ideal, or when competing against tough competitors. Coaches describe confident athletes as continuing to play hard, not giving up, and seeking out ways to get to the level they want. Confident athletes are able to get out of a down period quickly – accepting that failure can happen with new challenges – and it's okay. These athletes make challenges a part of becoming their best by welcoming those challenges.

As Pete Sampras said, "People wrote me off, but I believed in myself. I got the confidence back, and it grew and grew."

Types of Confidence

Sports psychologists explain that an athlete's overall confidence actually comes from a variety of sources, and that it is a boon to an athlete's best performance to identify his or her individual sources and focus on them. Take a concrete, focused approach rather than conceiving confidence as an overall feeling or abstract thought. The types of confidence are naturally very specific and unique to the individual, the particular sport, and the situation at the particular time.

Sports authorities describe the process of building confidence. It involves identifying sources of confidence and building from the bottom up, so to speak. Build a solid foundation that will ensure consistent, robust confidence in performance. For example, if a penalty kick taker considers the confidence sources he needs before attempting a penalty kick, he'll focus on several different types of confidence: in his technical ability for good contact, his past success with penalty taking, his ability for accuracy in placement, his ability to beat the opposing goal keeper, and his ability to handle pressure, as well as his ability to keep his energy up and his perception of his team's faith in him.

So to build his confidence in this particular regard, the penalty kick taker can focus his practice on his technical ability for good contact, his clear understanding of what is required for good contact, his positive self-statements about his ability to execute in the kick, his successful training experiences of this that he achieved at a high level, his successful technical contact with the ball consistently, positive coach feedback, and positive mental imagery of the event with an imagined feel of the ball making excellent contact.

Research by Vealey and Chase recently supported these types of confidence, labeling them physical, psychological, perceptual, physical fitness and training status, and ability to improve one's skill. Furthermore, they reported that for mastery and elite athletic success, *resilient* confidence was required, an unshakable self-belief.

Kerrin Lee-Gartner, Olympic champion alpine skier, described her experience of her own confidence level. "I was really confident," said Gartner. "I knew I was good enough, that if I put everything together, I could win. But I wasn't really thinking that. I was thinking how I would put it all together. The focus is so clear that you shut your thoughts off and you trust yourself and believe in yourself. You've already prepared for years and years. All you do is go, it's very natural."

Courage

The cowardly lion developed his courage from gaining confidence in himself and an award medal followed. That progression of events has been proven repeatedly by studies in sports psychology. Being fearful is a normal and necessary part of developing courage. As Arnold Schwarzenegger said, "Courage is about doing what you're afraid to do. There can be no courage unless you're scared."

Many other sports greats talk about courage:

"You've got to have the guts not be afraid to screw up. The guys who win are the ones who are not afraid to mess up." –Eddie Rickenbacker.

"Courage is not the absence of fear. It is being afraid but being able to control that fear so you are able to perform at your highest ability. That's what makes a champion." –Picabo Street

"To uncover your true potential you must first find your own limits, and then you have the courage to blow past them." –Frank "Fuzzy" Zeller, Jr.

Courage has historically been viewed as a part of one's excellent character. But today, courage is often viewed as a particular action with a successful outcome. A number of studies have looked at the various concepts about courage. Park and Peterson described it as an emotional strength, the will to be successful in reaching a goal when faced with opposition. Courage consists of bravery, perseverance, integrity, honesty, and zesty vitality.

Mavroudes explained that courage is a selfless pursuit of a moral good even when it involves risking personal harm. In discussion, he claimed courage is inversely related to knowledge – less courage is needed if the person has more knowledge, whereas more courage is necessary with little knowledge.

Fear and Courage

Studies on fear and courage that have described the role fear plays – fear's importance or relevance -- in the context of courage.

Woodward and Pury developed a Courage Scale-23 in which they found that fear may not necessarily be part of courage – it involves predominantly the willingness to act in a variety of context situations.

A Sports Specific Courage Model developed by Erkut Konter in 2004 includes interactions between the following factors that produce courage: risk, danger, fear at present, personal differences, personality traits, experience and knowledge, task at hand, and the particular sport. These definitions acknowledge that fear may or may not be present to any significant degree for an act to be considered courageous.

In a more recent published study on the development of a Sport Courage Scale, however, Konter did not include the fear requirement, determining courage to be a "natural and developed interaction and perceptual concept between person and situation and the task at hand that enables the person to move in competence, mastery, determination, assertiveness, venturesomeness, and altruistic behavior on a voluntary basis and in dangerous circumstances." The idea is that courage is not fearlessness, but coping with fear.

Konter's Sport Courage Scale

The Konter Sport Courage Scale revealed five factors as part of courage.

The first factor is determination. The word determination comes from Latin, meaning "limiting." Determination is the part of one's personality that would push on despite limits or barriers. Examples of determination would be "I perform to my best ability no matter the conditions, even under pressure," or "I always have my goals in sight."

The second factor is confidence and mastery. Confidence is described as the belief an athlete has that he or she can perform a desired behavior successfully. In sports, mastery is related to the performance of a skill and to the level of accomplishment. Confidence is a major part of mastery.

The third factor is assertiveness, described as using acceptable physical force with no intent to injure with an unusually high degree of effort to achieve a goal. An example of this would be "I like to take the initiative when faced with difficulties, and I assert myself even when facing dangerous situations."

The fourth factor is venturesomeness, or coping with fear and risk taking. In high-level sports, risk-taking behavior should be present. One researcher described sports as a culture of risks with acceptance of playing through the possibility of pain or injury, and coping with fear in the face of high risk or danger. Exercise in itself is a type of health risk management. An athlete might say, "I risk injury so that I won't lose," or "I perform my best even in the face of injury."

The fifth factor is sacrifice behaviors, or altruism. Players would say, "I do not hesitate to compete even when faced with possible defeat," or "I defend my beliefs even if this action could be harmful to me."

Whether or not fear enters it, athletes who have broken records have been shown in another study to be described as courageous by taking high risks when challenged by strong opponents in an event or competitive event that was stressful.

Commitment

A recent study at the University of Ottawa to investigate the qualities of exceptional performers in sports determined that the first element of excellence, that which allows the person to become the best, is commitment and belief. The researchers described commitment as "the heart of human excellence, the overall perspective, the way one views the self, and the capacity for importance of the pursuit and desire to become the best."

Commitment in this study is equated with passion, hard work, persistence in the face of obstacles, and the belief in yourself and what you do. The study delineated five other elements as essential to exceptional performance in sports, and these five were described as skills that channel commitment and belief into actions that make for that top performance. The five supporting elements are full focus, positive images, mental readiness, distraction control, and constructive evaluation.

As Larry Cain, Olympic champion in canoeing, said, "Everything I do, whether it is weights, or running, or the normal training things, or the leisure activities I do, is all geared toward how it's going to affect my performance. Everything is opportunity/cost. If I go out to a movie instead of going hiking as my leisure activity, what is the cost of that? If I go to the movies instead of a hike, does that help or hurt my performance? I've got to judge that. I have always dreamed about being the best in the world."

Kerrin Lee-Gartner, Olympic champion in alpine skiing said, "It's (being) committed through the ups and downs. Committed through the good results and the bad results, when you're coming in 50th and it looks like there's never an end to the bad results. You still have to be committed and still focused and still trying to win every race. I think the day that you let your commitment go is the day you don't have a chance to win."

In the University of Ottawa study, researchers described commitment as the first essential ingredient guiding the pursuit of excellence. It is about committing the self to be the best you can be and continually working to make improvement to persist through ups and downs to maintain the best performance. It's a commitment to the goal of excelling which ignites and drives you daily to act in ways that lead to excelling. This means committing to high quality mental, physical, and technical preparation, clear goals, relentless pursuit of them, and always training smart with adequate recovery for regeneration.

The requirement for this level of excellence is also committing to a positive balance between training and performance and quality rest and relaxation for adequate balance. This means respecting individual needs.

Strengthening Commitment

Coaches and sports therapists agree that commitment is strengthened when the athletes believes he or she is investing in something worthwhile, like the people and organization linked with pursuit of the goal, and knowing those people value and support and believe in you. Commitment nurtures belief in the self and your potential, and that in turn strengthens commitment to the goal. Clearly, there is a symbiotic relationship between commitment and confidence.

Suggested Questions to Ask Yourself to Determine Your Level of Commitment

- Are your goals clear, challenging, and targeted at being your best?

- Do you work at improving something each day at every practice or performance?

- Will your commitment to training be enough to take you to your high-level goals?

- Is your commitment to respecting your personal needs for balance, rest, recovery, and nutrition strong enough to reach your goals?

Committed or Courageous or Confident?

Who could ever forget the recent feat of 64-year-old U.S. endurance swimmer Diana Nyad, who became the first person to swim from Cuba to Florida without a shark cage? Nyad said, as she completed her 53-hour journey, "I have three messages. One is, we should never, ever give up. Two is, you're never too old to chase your dream. Three is, it looks like a solitary sport, but it is a team." She also said, "The harder you work, the harder it is to surrender."

Traditionally, there has been too much emphasis placed on confidence alone as the primary characteristic of successful athletes. However, today the winningest coaches and true champions agree that confidence without both commitment and courage is like a high-performance Indy car without any fuel in the gas tank. It may look like a winner, but it won't get very far. Seeing success as the triangle formed from the Three Cs – with confidence as the base and commitment and courage as the supporting sides – helps an athlete stay in great "shape" and keeps an athlete pointed in the right direction.

CHAPTER 7

MENTAL TOUGHNESS – TRAIN YOUR BRAIN FOR PEAK PERFORMANCE

What we witness in athletics – in person or on TV – is an amazing show of physical bodies performing feats we could only dream about. But interestingly enough, top sports psychologists, sports researchers, coaches, and the athletes themselves credit not their muscles, but their minds with their peak performances and successes.

Here are just a few lines from some well-known personalities in sports.

- "The pool is terrible, but that doesn't have much to do with my record swims. That's all mental attitude." –Mark Spitz

- "I've been in a poor physical shape many times in my career and I've had some of my best results. My best performances happened because my mind was in the right place. The mind is definitely stronger than the body." –Kelly Slater

- "When I'm down or maybe when it's close in the match, I feel like I'm still in it. I don't feel like I'm letting down. Mentally, I'm still really, really tough." –Maria Sharapova

- "The ideal attitude is to be physically loose and mentally tight." –Arthur Ashe

- "The thing about the game at this level [MLB] is that there is very little difference in physical skills between players; the real difference between them is upstairs. It is what is 'in your head' that makes the difference." –Cletis "Clete" Boyer

- "Once you're physically capable of winning a gold medal, the rest is 90 percent mental." –Patti Johnson

- "What you are thinking, what shape your mind is in, is what makes the biggest difference of all." –Willie Mays

- "Players today put too much emphasis on lifting weights, low body fat, and big muscles, that they think make them look good – all that's b.s. What you need to play hockey is heart and determination, and the ability to stay mentally strong. Mental strength beats physical strength any day." –Phil Esposito

- "Your toughness is made up of equal parts persistence and experience. You don't so much outrun your opponents as outlast and outsmart them, and the toughest opponent of all is the one inside your head." –Joe Henderson

If only it were possible to read the minds of athletes as they do their thing; maybe their mindfulness would be contagious. But are the mental processes of successful athletes actually hard to see? The media loves celebrities who screw up, so we all hear about the setbacks of the likes of Tiger Woods, Michael Jordan, and Wayne Gretzky. Yet we have seen, and still see, that not a single one was wiped off the face of the earth, but instead showed an amazing mental toughness in their ability to triumph, even when facing the immense pressures of their setbacks and adversity.

From the Projects to the Pros (Preparation is the Key)

When I think about mental toughness, every aspect of the game is involved. One example I will use has to do with time and weather conditions. The majority of the games that I played in the NFL were either at 1 p.m. or 3 p.m. With that in mind, when I was conditioning and training, I would do it at the hottest time of the day, which is around the same time as the games. I can remember, during the off season, running Arrowhead Stadium steps in the mid-afternoon and doing all my cardio training then. In my mind, it only made sense that if you are going to play that time of the day, your body better be conditioned to perform at your peak at that time. It goes back to what I've been saying: it's not just the physical, but the mental aspect that is involved because you know that the majority of players have a different mindset.

In that respect, there was no doubt in my mind that I could play 60 minutes at peak performance and hope my opponents are doing the complete opposite. I could see this with my mind's eye!

When I think about somebody else whose mental toughness had an impact on me personally, I'd have to go with a guy by the name of Pat Etcheberry. He was my strength and conditioning coach at the University of Kentucky. He is one of the world's foremost experts in the field of sports fitness and movement. He has been the head trainer at the University of Kentucky and trained professional athletes in a wide variety of sports including tennis, golf, and football. Etcheberry's clients have won more than 90 Grand Slam tournaments, people like Justine Henin, Pete Sampras, Jim Courier, Monica Seles, Martina Hingis, and Jelena Jankovic. A former Olympian in javelin competition in 1964 in the Tokyo Games, Etcheberry has trained fifteen Olympic medalists. He is the director of the Etcheberry Sports Performance Division at the Saddlebrook Resort in Tampa, Florida where he develops both world-class professionals and aspiring players as young as eight years old in a variety of sports.

During the off season in college, our conditioning program was designed to improve our overall physical conditioning. Emphasis was placed upon increasing muscle mass, strength, speed, endurance. and agility. This off-season conditioning program was divided into two seasons: the winter program and the summer program. The mental aspect of our speed and endurance-type drills and weight training was so important in our overall conditioning. These training sessions were very intense, and visualization was a key piece of the puzzle that would take my athletic ability to the next level. The takeaway is that visualization is one of the key ingredients to the game of life.

Admiring the Athletes

One of the most amazing things about elite athletes is that they are always under severe stress and pressure to consistently perform at the top of their game, and they never give up. We always see them putting their bodies through pain and sweat to win and succeed. How do they put their minds and bodies through such rigorous, draining work? The top performers don't stop to think; they concentrate only on what is necessary for top performance. They call it mental toughness. But how do they do it? How do they persevere to be so successful?

A World Class Champion's Mental Answer

A world champion, national gold medalist, and Hall of Famer Lisa Brown credits her rise to the triumphant role of an "unstoppable" coach and mental toughness therapist to her ability to reimagine herself as an athlete. Brown humbly describes her younger self, choking at big events: "Even when I practiced and prepared with 100% intensity, I'd often find a way to choke in big events. Other times I'd start out totally confident, only to face problem after problem – such as a poor start, an opponent who was on fire, or bad officiating. Pretty soon, I'd get a sinking feeling in my stomach that today wasn't my day, and it would go downhill from there."

Luckily, she realized her failures were about her mental game, and she made it her mission to develop a program to transform her athletic life. Brown's mental toughness approach took years of research and testing with Olympic athletes. Today, that recipe for mental toughness includes how to psych up with unstoppable confidence before major games, developing the ability to cope under pressure, and bringing out natural courage to win under pressure when the circumstances are non-optimal. This is accomplished by recognizing three crippling mistakes that result in a loss of mental toughness and eliminating them.

Brown's Crippling Mistakes and How to Avoid Them

1. Pressure. We all feel pressure, and athletes, some might argue, do so more than most. Brown identifies ways to deal with the many different pressures athletes face. Rather than letting your good physical training take your body where it needs to go, you should begin to use your head to direct your body. Guiding, steering, and focusing on the opponent rather than on your own plan is helpful. Although it is natural to be a bit nervous, remaining emotionally calm is essential to success. Golf legend Babe Didrikson Zaharias is known to have said, "Luck? Sure, but only after long practice and only with the ability to think under pressure."

2. Personal Issues. There are personal demons that cause stress and adversely affect your confidence. Identify them and eliminate them. Brown cites André Agassi as an example. Agassi, who was a perfectionist, could not tolerate making an error that made him feel shame. He dealt with his personal issues, and was then able to perfect his abilities.

3. Self-Criticism. Over-criticizing your poor performances and setbacks only causes frustration. It is only human to make mistakes, and it is necessary to learn from them. Criticizing yourself leads to a lack of confidence, and saying "I can't do it" is very harmful to future success. When you feel that that you can't do something, you won't. Thankfully, the opposite is often true as well.

The Mental Edge

Successful coaches claim that mental toughness is the most important psychological skill for an athlete who wants to excel athletically. It is easy for anyone to overlook the mental work involved in sports, as the accuracy of the athlete and his or her ball-manipulating, play-making skills are easy to focus on, admire, and judge. Yet despite talent and amazing execution, the research of psychologists and coaches agrees that no matter the passion or skill, in order to reach the desired pinnacle of success, an athlete must successfully deal with the frustration that always comes about through sports, and that requires good mental training and mental toughness.

Legendary soccer manager Sven-Goran Eriksson said, "So little is required to be successful in a sport. It's certainly mostly a matter of psychology, and in the end, it's that psychological difference that decides whether you win or lose."

Kirk Mango, a national champion gymnast and three-time inductee into the Hall of Fame, claims he was not an exceptionally talented young athlete. He credits mental training for developing and shaping the attitude that propelled him to the top. "The mental game side is all about what the athlete believes. This belief is what makes the biggest difference in how athletes act. Attitude and belief about what one can accomplish are essential to any possibility of achieving anything."

Holistic life coach Dr. Tal Ben-Shahar claims that in order for an athlete in peak physical condition to achieve a higher level of performance and gain an edge over the competition, the athlete must experience an increase in mental performance. After peak physical condition is achieved, further progress is no longer a matter of physical skill, but rather a matter of how skillfully an athlete can develop and apply psychological skills.

Ben-Shahar describes a hierarchical pyramid of sports skills for peak performance. The foundation is attitude and motivation developed through practice with a mindset focused on growth. In the middle is a positive self-belief and awareness strengths. In the top level, skills involve managing emotions and resilience – the ability to deal with stress, setbacks, adversity, and changing situations, to adapt and learn from the situations, and to rise above the challenges and perform at the best possible level. This is the final stage of mental toughness.

Martina Hingis is quoted as saying, "I didn't have the same mindset or ability as the other girls, so I had to beat them with my mind." Hingis isn't a chess player, so how exactly does the mind work in the world of physically active sports and athletics?

Dr. Jason Silk, the Director of Mental Training for the St. Louis Cardinals and a featured TV personality, credits not only athletic success but also happiness and health to the process of strengthening the mind. Research shows that people who can control how they think live longer, happier, healthier, and more successful lives than those who are less mentally tough.

How Tough is Mental Toughness?

Army psychologists have recently aligned with sports psychologists, since they have similar plans for how to reach peak level performance. In sports, athletes need to become "psychological Teflon." Former army psychologist Dr. Bret A. Moore said that participants in both sports and the military are expected to perform at their peak. It's about being able to focus, weed out extraneous information, and concentrate on the task at hand.

Former Navy SEAL officer turned sports coach Stew Smith has recommendations for strengthening an athlete's will to succeed in the "combat" of sports. Smith's effective plan is:

1. The first step is to break down the big picture – which can be a big obstacle – into fragments or sub-goals. For example, Smith offers that endurance athletes should see a marathon as a series of one-mile circuits, and a football player should only be involved with the next down rather than the entire game. Thinking about the big picture actually slows you down.

2. It is important to isolate the feelings that motivate the task. To do this, you must consider the motivation and the thinking that you need in order to perform the specific task at hand, and you need to use a verbal cue or keyword to remind you of a time when you performed that

task perfectly. When you use a verbal cue, it draws you right into the same feeling and energy that you experienced when you first performed the task perfectly. Your reflexes take over, and the necessary decision making is instantaneous. When the keyword is used over and over, the repetition creates brain shortcuts, which means that eventually, Smith's technique requires less thinking. The body just reacts, which leaves less opportunity to choke or delay. Smith's plan of simulation in this manner is highly effective in both military and sports, and he calls it "planning the dive and diving the plan."

3. The final step is utilizing proper breathing techniques. Inhaling and exhaling large breaths is a skill that slows down the system and metabolizes adrenaline, which causes you to think clearly. "The Mental Workout," by Jason Selk, explains a 15-second centering breath of 6:2:7. Breathe in for six seconds, hold for two, and breathe out for seven. Selk's breathing technique helps to control your heart rate, which can help control your arousal state and positively affect your ability to think under pressure.

Smith's techniques are a formal part of the Army's curriculum.

More Soldier/Athlete Workouts for Mental Muscle

As a trainer for the Comprehensive Soldier Fitness Performance and Resilience Enhancement program, Melanie Mousseau explains that an athlete's elite performance has its roots in sports psychology. Her program, which was first designed for Olympic athletes, is used for army and civilian life as well. Mousseau explains that her program focuses on teaching an important lesson: thoughts greatly influence performance. Mousseau's plan consists of several steps. The first step is for the athlete to acknowledge his or her skills and deficiencies; the athlete must come to a complete understanding of what they are capable of and recognize all of the possible deterrents. The athlete must then work on how to improve these hindrances through thoughts, which Mousseau claims is the most influential factor. After this, the athlete can begin working on a seven-step program.

Step 1: Think carefully. In order to build confidence, it is important to not dwell on your past or present failures. Instead, look at your successes, and pay attention to what makes up the successes, such as motivation and skill.

Step 2: Focus your attention. It is important to control your attention using a verbal cue or keyword that will keep you in the moment. It is crucial to focus on what is important to succeed, and not focus on unrelated problems. Successful athletes block any and all unimportant thoughts that are not related to succeeding in the moment.

Step 3: Regulate your energy. Conserving energy is an important aspect of every sport and an effective way to regulate energy is through breathing. Using proper breathing techniques will lead to a peak mental state, as well as help you conserve energy. You don't want to waste energy, since you never know when you will need it most.

Step 4: Set your goals. Have the mental strength to plan the goals in a systematic way, and persevere to execute them despite barriers and challenges. With small milestones, what can seem unrealistic can be easily achieved.

Step 5: Visualize. Using imagery with all of your senses to create a scene in your mind will keep you focused. While in training, Mousseau has participants see themselves achieving their goals.

The most important thing is to put a mental toughness plan into action, to actually exercise and utilize it. As long-distance runner Lynn Jennings said, "Mental will is a muscle that needs exercise, just like muscles of the body."

Sports Psychology Supported by the Mind

Sports psychologists, coaches, and athletes have found in recent years that winning championships is not just about excelling in skills and physical performance, but is equally dependent on mental preparation and psychological strength. Sports psychologists emphasize that it is actually mental toughness that forms the core of sports success.

The importance of mental toughness is due to stress and anxiety on the athlete. Sports psychologist G. Jones referred to stress and anxiety as "a state that results from the demands that are placed on the individual which require that person to engage in some coping behavior. Anxiety results when the individual doubts his or her ability to cope with the situation that causes stress." For athletes, the pressure to consistently succeed adds to the pressure, stress, and anxiety.

A recent study defined mental toughness as the ability to perform at optimal level no matter what the circumstances may be. The study showed that changing an athlete's mental state also results in a change in his or her physical state, either consciously or subconsciously. This is important, because when anxiety and tension cause muscle tension, it interferes with performance. Tension compromises nerves and leads to less coordinated muscle movement, which makes it difficult to perform coordinated muscle actions.

Why Anxiety and Stress Zaps Performance Ability

When an athlete experiences anxiety, they can have two reactions: the fight reaction, which is excitement, and is motivated by the challenge, and there is the more common response, which is the flight reaction. The flight reaction causes the athlete to focus on the negative aspects of the performance.

Damaging Thoughts

Recent brain-mapping studies have shown that just thinking about failure actually suppresses the brain's ability to perform, and this is detrimental to an athlete's success. The brain can sabotage the body very easily.

Brad "One Punch" Pickett, a mixed martial arts athlete, is quoted as saying, "Focus on your performance, not victory. I used to be so fixated on winning the fight I used to think that no matter what happens, I have go to win, and I piled so much pressure on myself. Now I just want to perform the best I can."

And How the Tough Get Going

A research study from the *International Journal of Sport Psychology* showed how mental toughness contributes to performance and thinking. Participants in static cycling trials were categorized as having either high low levels of mental toughness. The study showed that those having high mental toughness perceived that they put in significantly less exertion at the maximum intensity level than participants in the low mental toughness group. Researchers offered that "when the going gets tough, the tough get going," and explained that tough-minded individuals might perceive themselves as being in control of the situation, and they see the intensity as a challenge instead of a threat. As football player Alex Karras said, "Toughness is in the soul and spirit, not in muscles."

Reaching the Competitive Advantage

There are established sports psychology centers that work specifically with all levels of serious athletes on learning and sharpening the mental skills that are recognized as necessary for a competitive advantage. One such center, the Ohio Center for Sport Psychology, describes working with nine mental skills:

1. Choose and maintain a positive attitude, and be open to learning from both success and failure. Reach for excellence, not perfection, and maintain a respect for the balance in life.

2. Be aware that your desired rewards may come from participation and not outcome. Maintain a high level of self-motivation that will help you work through barriers and challenges, even when the rewards are not immediate.

3. Set high but realistic goals with commitment to reaching the goals through daily demands of training.

4. Deal effectively with people.

5. Use positive self-talk as a way to keep your self-confidence going, and regulate thoughts, feelings, and behaviors.

6. Use positive mental imagery and memories of performing well in competitions for preparation, and also to recover from poor performances.

7. Manage anxiety effectively.

8. Manage emotions effectively so that performance is improved rather than hindered.

9. Maintain concentration with focus, resist distractions, and regain focus if it is lost in a competition.

The skills are also organized into three levels: Level 1 contains the skills that are used daily for learning and practice and are necessary for long-term goals. Level 2 skills are used to prepare for performance. Finally, Level 3 skills are used during the actual performance.

Contrary to what you might think looking at all the heavy lifting in the weight rooms of most gyms, true strength training is not about your muscles, but about your mind. In any sport or endeavor, mental focus contributes more to peak performance than any physical training. Martial arts master Bruce Lee said it best: "As you think, so shall you become."

SECTION III

GETTING CENTERED

CHAPTER 8

TIPS AND TECHNIQUES – SELF-TALK, VISUALIZATION, BREATHING, RELAXATION

What goes on in your center? Is your head chatter overwhelming your center, especially during crucial performance moments?

Centering is a necessary action to take in this world of stressful events, events that particularly affect athletic performance. Stress and anxiety rob good energy from your mind and body and prevent you from adequately using energy in the first place. Centering is utilizing techniques that can release your stress and anxiety and keep you balanced in the present.

Originating in the Japanese martial art Aikido, the idea of centering originally meant "the way of unifying life energy," and more specifically, unifying the energy within yourself. There are techniques which can be used to control, manage, and master your head chatter and stress reactions. These techniques can be used to make sure that the stress doesn't master you; they keep you focused on the moment so that your inner strengths are not compromised.

Dr. Caroline Leaf said that people have over 30,000 thoughts per day, and most of those thoughts are uncontrolled. So how can you control your thoughts? How can you catch yourself if you have negative thoughts about fears that influence the direction for your life?

From the Projects to the Pros (Finding What Works for You)

A lot of players have certain rituals that they have to do before a game. My ritual was not to do the same thing over and over; for example, how I got dressed, what time I arrived for the game, which sock I put on first, and so on. My ritual was joking around. This was my way of calming my nerves and taking my mind off of the game. With all the preparation the week of the game, along with my psychological edge (nutrition) file, practice, conditioning, meeting, and team game plan, I didn't want to overthink or cause any more stress for the task at hand. That is what took place in the locker room. Once I was the field, before the game started, I had my pre-visualization come into play. Preparation was the foundation throughout the game, whether I performed according to plan or made a mistake. I would replay what I did right or wrong to correct or improve.

Along with this, breathing slowly when visualizing helped me to calm down and to recover from any negative things going on with myself of the team. In basketball terms, rebound!

Chatter that Takes You Off Center and Off Balance

The thoughts that occur in the minds of athletes can be positive or negative chatter, and the negative chatter causes stress. "The biggest source of stress for an athlete is their personal expectations and the expectations of others," said Peter Crocker, professor of sport and exercise psychology at UBC's school of kinesiology. Sports psychologists are now regularly helping athletes deal with these pressures with the tools of self-talk, visualization, relaxation, and breathing.

Sports psychologist for Olympic athletes Dr. Wayne Halliwell advises athletes to own the moment, because as he explains, the most important task for Olympic athletes is to not think about past races. Halliwell's counseling brings about a calm relaxation and spurs on the combination of mind, body, and spirit that is necessary for balance.

Halliwell uses mantras, keywords, and self-talk to help athletes learn how to focus and succeed. "Why not me?" is one mantra that he often recommends. Gold medalist swimmer Mark Tewksbury uses some of the techniques recommended by Halliwell: keywords and self-talk. Keywords are positive, personally chosen words such as the aforementioned "Why not me?" and they work when athletes repeat the words to themselves. It's a planned form of optimism which helps them focus on their performance instead of focusing on the crowd, judges, and other competitors.

Olympic gold medal skier Jennifer Heil revealed that going into the games ranked as a favorite added great pressures to her performance. Dr. Halliwell explained that pressures such as Heil's often cause athletes to perform poorly. Hallowell's techniques to control emotions help to eliminate stress and enable the athlete to always perform at their peak.

Tom Hall, an Olympic canoe racer, utilized self-talk along with visualization during his training. "I sat in a chair with my head down and visualized the race," Hall said. "I used my key words, focused on myself and the job I wanted to do."

Gold medal runner Joan Benoit Samuelson used similar techniques and described her experience while racing Ingrid Kristiansen. "I kept surging ahead, but Ingrid would always respond. I couldn't seem to shake her. I had prepared mentally for the race by using imagery. During the marathon, I would see myself running easily on my favorite ten-mile loop. Then I would picture myself on a six-mile loop followed by another ten-mile trail run. Dividing it up in my mind that way made the race seem shorter and more enjoyable."

Centering for Being in the Zone

Much has been written about "being in the zone," which is that ideal state where everything clicks perfectly, as if without effort, or even consciousness.

Coaches and sports therapists often counsel that the process of getting into the zone is simplified when an athlete recognizes what type of mental arousal they experience and how it helps or hinders performance. Many athletes have excessive arousal; they become too keyed up, which can lead to muscle tension, difficulties in concentration, decision making, unbalanced or uncoordinated rhythm, and choking in performance. Centering is a recognized technique that can benefit an athlete's control and help her or him maintain the balance essential for getting into the zone.

The Pre-Performance Centering

The idea of centering was first conceived by sports psychologist Dr. Robert Nideffer, and it was initially used by Olympic psychologist Dr. Don Greene in the 1970s. The technique was designed to channel nerves in the most productive manner to help the athlete direct and maintain focus, poise, and calm, quieting the brain's unproductive head chatter. Sometimes this process is understood as learning to use the creative, dynamic, and inspired right brain rather than left brain, which is described as being overly analytical and critical thinking-oriented.

Sports therapists often quip, "You can't stop the waves, but you can learn to surf," while recommending centering techniques.

7 Steps for Centering

The process for centering entails seven steps.

1. Find a comfortable focal point in front of you below your eye level. Keeping a focal point can you help avoid distractions.

2. Have a clear intention when you perform or play. Put your intentions into a positive statement, focusing on what you want rather than what you don't want. For example, "I will perform at my peak with passion and clear focus," instead of "Don't strike out."

3. Mindful breathing has proven to be a powerful technique for controlling stress. Diaphragmatic breathing is not just efficient, but activates the parasympathetic nervous system response in the body which helps to regulate the fight or flight response.

4. Take note of any muscle tension and use techniques to release the tension. Scan your muscles one muscle group at a time while breathing slowly to release tension on the exhale.

5. Locate your center and "life force." There is a location in the body where energy is believed to be stored, and that is the human center of gravity. The Eastern term "chi" is described as this center; locating it will place you in a sense of balance, grace, and calm. Sports psychologists counsel that the act of finding your center will help to quiet your head chatter.

6. Use a sensory word or phrase to remind you of the feelings related to what you want to accomplish or how you want to perform. The ideal word is personally chosen, and can be something like fluid, powerful, smooth-stroke, or even-shifts. The chosen word should give you a mental sound, feeling, or image of an exact performance. Alternatively, imagery alone can be used without any accompanying words or phrases, as long as the image reminds you of succeeding.

7. Channel your energy. Gather your energy from your center and direct it upward like a surge of brilliance through your eyes or head.

Practice is Key to Centering

Sports therapists recommend that you practice centering techniques for 10-15 minutes a day when first starting out. The therapists say that you should notice a difference in performance in one to two weeks, and soon, centering will only take a few seconds!

Imagery/Visualization

Imagery is the powerhouse means of inner communication. Visualizations are positive images that are specifically used to affect how the body responds to a particular situation. They are detailed reenactments in the mind of activities in which you picture yourself performing at your peak. These images are used to enhance an athletes training. Imagery can also be used to coax the mind into being flexible and allows you to be able to shift gears to properly handle an immediate situation or task.

Imagery is often used along with self-talk and breathing, but it is considered by sports therapists and athletes to be more efficient than self-talk. For example, just think of how difficult it is and how long it would take to describe a perfect swimming stroke in words. Now that you've done that, think about how relatively simple it would be to picture an image of Michael Phelps doing the same stroke.

Sports psychologists agree on the value of visualization. One psychologist has recommended that a minute of visualization is worth seven minutes of practice! This is due to the fact that through proper visualization, you will feel ready to perform at your highest potential.

Because imagery allows you to both pre-experience and re-experience quality performance, it becomes a guide for your actions and gives you feelings of control, as well as a particularly high-quality body-mind connection.

A Vision in Your Head

Here are some tips for visualizing:

- Use your eyes as your camera. Picture your scene, paying attention to all of your senses, and use as many details as possible. Visualize the entire scene. Begin with the warm-up and finish with the buzzer.

- Take note of your feelings when you see yourself doing your best, being successful, and winning.

- If something goes wrong, replay your scene and fix it.

- Feel free to picture your scene repeatedly at any speed you'd like!

- The more you repeat this technique, the stronger and more trained your mind-body experience will be.

Visualization simulates a perfect performance, and this serves to train the neuromuscular system. Recent studies have shown that visualization improves physical performance because the mind learns just as much from a visualized experience as it does from an actual experience. These studies have also shown that mental visualization results in the most positive successes when it is used before practice or competition. Mental visualization will improve performance as seen in studies, even without physical activity.

Why Does Mental Visualization Work?

An athlete will create an accurate visualization of a perfect performance, and this simulation will train the neuromuscular system to learn how to achieve the perfect performance. The human mind can't distinguish between a real and a visualized experience.

Mental Rehearsal by Visualizing

Mental rehearsing was recognized by Russian Olympic athletes in the 1980s as a way to make a positive difference in their overall performance. Recently, research has confirmed that even five minutes of mental visualization makes a significant difference in performance. Other research has shown that mental rehearsal or visualization affects the autonomic nervous system; visualization creates a brain pattern that the muscles will follow.

Visualizing the Scene

Coaches and sports therapists agree that imagery can build confidence and motivation, but in order to really be effective, athletes must recognize the skills they need to work on, the same way they would when playing. An athlete needs to be an active participant, not just passive viewer.

Studies have shown that imagery is most effective when you visualize a process, the step by step procedure necessary to achieve your goal or play, rather than the end goal. Sports psychologists explain that you must imagine yourself putting in the work and performing each step, each movement, and each action necessary to get that medal and achieve that goal rather than simply seeing yourself holding the medal.

Visualize – see yourself in the place you perform, just as it is in the real world. Use all of your senses; hear the sounds, smell the arena, taste the water, see the track, touch your equipment. In your mind, you are watching yourself, but you need to do more than just watch, you need to experience. Put as much detail into your visualization as possible. The more detailed that you can make this, the better your mind and body will know how to duplicate it in the real world.

As you go through each step, the process will eventually become second nature. Practice or rehearse 15-20 minutes a day. Sports coaches attest that with a few minutes of visualization practice a day, there will be improvements by the end of the week.

Beginning a Visualization

Many sports therapists recommend beginning visualization with a relaxation exercise. Relaxation exercises help you get into a focused and clear state.

Visualization is touted by coaches, athletes, and sports psychologists as a helpful mental rehearsal, and when athletes face any situation in real time, their minds and bodies already have the imprinted response to handle any situation in the most effective manner possible.

Olympic athlete Thomas Hall credits his success overcoming underdog status to his regular practice of visualization as a mental rehearsal.

Breathing – the Core of Body Harmony

Breathing controls all of the other functions of your body and helps you to maintain balance. Through maintaining an awareness of your breathing, you can learn to use it as a focusing aid. Research has shown that through utilizing proper breathing techniques, you can take control of your body, mind, and the emotions that need kept in check in order to accomplish any pursuit. Yes, we all breathe, but not necessarily efficiently. The more efficiently you breathe, the more oxygen you breathe in, and the more oxygen that you breathe in, the less you need to use glycogen supplies (glycogen is a type of glucose in your body that gives you energy).

Former champion long-distance runner and current coach Alberto Salazar explained, "I'd speed up or somebody surged, I'd find my breathing really out of sync. You have to relax and get it back to a level where it is natural, where you don't have to think about it again. You've got to concentrate on relaxing. It's hard, but that's what athletics is. You have to find that natural cadence that you have and stay relaxed within that cadence."

Maintaining awareness of your breathing and knowing how to arrive at a place of focused relaxation will help you to avoid stress. Awareness of your breathing brings focus, and even if you can only focus on the current breath, you aren't distracted while you are breathing. This means that you are shielded from anxieties that stem from past or future fears. You are tuned in to the task at hand. You may even be propelled into the zone – those moments of perfection and harmony, a perfect balance of mind, body, and emotions.

Breathing can help eliminate the distractions of head chatter that hold you back from success. Practicing proper breathing techniques prepares you for using them whenever you need to – whenever there is annoying or debilitating head chatter.

Studies have shown that breathing awareness increases your energy level. Performance and efficiency can improve 10% or more.

Another Simple Breathing Routine

Sit down, take a deep breath in, and just focus on letting the air fill you up. After you've done this, exhale slowly through your mouth. Focus on a positive thought. Focus on what you want to achieve with an affirmation like, "success, confidence, mine." Spend a few seconds focusing on your breathing, and while you are breathing, find your physical center of gravity, just a little below your waist. This part of your body centers, stabilizes, and grounds you. So when you feel stress, pressure, or head chatter, focusing on the feeling of your center will remind you of balance and control.

Self-Talk

What thoughts are you focusing on? Are they telling you certain things? Your mind is very powerful and will influence your actions, performance, and accomplishments. Sometimes, the thoughts that you focus on can be about failures, obstacles, fears, and other negative things. Catching all of your negative thoughts can help an athlete – or anyone, for that matter – get rid of them and replace the negatives with positives.

A recent study has shown just how efficient words and phrases are at helping to improve performance. In the study published in *Medicine and Science in Sports and Exercise*, a group of cyclists rode for as long as possible at 80% of peak power and their times were recorded. After this, they were divided into two groups, one of which was instructed to use positive self-talk. This group chose four positive statements including "feeling good, drive forward, push ahead, work it," and they were taught to use the positive phrases in a mental training session. The other group did nothing extra. Both groups were retested after a two-week period. Results showed that the cyclists who used self talk improved their time and actually dropped their perceived exertion levels, while the control group had no change in either effort or time. The self-talk group reported that they felt like they weren't working as hard or as long!

Just as this study proved, finding your own key words or mantras will be effective at improving your athletic efforts. Self-talk can boost positive motivation; you can be your very own cheerleading section. Andre Agassi wrote about his own self-talk. "For me, the self-talk starts here in the afternoon shower. This is when I begin to say things to myself, crazy things, over and over, until I believe them. For instance, that a quasi-cripple (me) can compete at the U.S. Open. That a thirty-six-year-old man can beat an opponent just entering his prime. I've won 869 matches in my career, fifth on the all-time list, and many were won during the afternoon shower."

The Power of Positive Self-Talk

Doubts can wreck your confidence. When you discover any doubts that you have, turn them into positive affirmations and use them in your self-talk. For example: "I can do this, I will finish strong, trust my training, and play hard. I am a strong hitter; I have strong mental skills." Sports therapists recommend six to ten good affirmations for positive self-talk, and they recommend that you practice them daily in order for them to pervade your thinking. Eventually, positive affirmations will come automatically and will help to keep you in balance.

When to Do It

Dr. Nicole Kulikov, sports psychologist and marathoner, is an expert on the importance of using imagery and self-talk as part of regular practice sessions. Kulikov explained that many athletes make the mistake of only using imagery and self-talk immediately before and during competitions. In order for these techniques to be effective, self-talk and visualizing should become a habit used to enhance training, a method of eliminating fears and obstacles that threaten to inhibit your performance.

The Use and Value of Self Talk

A meta-analysis of 32 sports psychology studies published in *Perspectives on Psychological Science* confirmed that self-talk contributes significant changes in athletic performance. The study pointed out which particular types of self-talk were most beneficial for specific tasks. The two types of self talk are instructional and motivational:

Instructional self-talk was shown to be more beneficial than motivational self-talk for improving techniques for improving specific skills. For example, it is more effective for a golfer to use specific body reminders such as "swing with your hips," rather than "atta boy, you can do it."

Motivational self-talk was determined to be more effective for boosting confidence, excitement, and for tasks of strength and endurance. For instance, thoughts such as, "you can do it, let's go get them" are positive thoughts and have proven to boost confidence.

Another significant value of self-talk is that it helps with learning a task. Self-talk helps through repetition.

Antonis Hatzigeorgiadis, sports psychologist of the Department of Physical Education and Sport Sciences at the University of Thessaly, said of this study, "The mind guides action. If we succeed in regulating our thoughts, then this will help our behavior."

Carl Lewis, track and field gold medalist, is one of many who has used self-talk with successful results. As Lewis said, "My thoughts before a big race are usually pretty simple. I tell myself: get out of the blocks, run your race, stay relaxed. If you run your race, you'll win. Channel your energy. Focus."

Relaxation

Relaxation is a technique that sports therapists and coaches use to cope with pressure, which in turn affects the ability to focus, center, and maintain balance. One method of physical relaxation is progressive muscular relaxation. Studies have shown that this technique benefits performance through reducing anxiety.

Relaxation – Benefit or Hindrance?

While It is true that athletes need to be "pumped up" before a game, the value of relaxation cannot be ignored.

Relaxation benefits the athlete's ability to implement visualization and self-talk – allowing the athlete to be more open to positive ideas, thus further enhancing performance. However, while you may need to be relaxed to perform at your peak, what if you find that you must be fired up to experience motivation? The first step is to know which type of performance arousal works best for you and implement it into your personal routine. For optimal performance, discover when you are most efficient and work it to your advantage, using your skills and potential.

Relaxation Techniques

One great relaxation exercise is the 100 breaths meditation.

This technique begins with a five-minute body stretch, spending 20 seconds on each of the large muscle groups. Do an upward stretch: arms high, palms facing the sky. This stretch will lengthen the spine. Then slowly twist the torso. Next, touch your toes and stretch out your back. Extend your arms to the front and keep them parallel. This will stretch the back and open the chest. Next, stretch the leg muscles by entering a squat position, and lean forward, place your hands on your knees, and press your knees down. When you've entered the final stage of this stretch, sit down and keep your spine straight.

This is when the breathing exercises come into play. While sitting, let your shoulders sag. Focus your eyes about three inches below your navel while inhaling and exhaling deeply through your nose. Feel the air traveling into your nose and moving into your lungs; then follow your breath back up and out. Focus your attention on your breathing. Be aware of it through your senses, the sounds and feelings. Remain in this position and count 100 breaths.

During this count, you'll find yourself thinking instead of counting – but this is normal thinking, not negative thinking. This thinking is inspired by pictures or dialogues from the past. Just acknowledge that you are thinking, end the thought, and begin counting again. The more you practice this, the less frustrating your uncontrolled thoughts will be. You will find it easier and easier to relax yourself at any time.

Don't worry about the time while you're breathing. You might start out faster, but as you relax your breaths will slow. Breathing can vary from 8-12 breaths per minute to between 4-8 breaths a minute during relaxation time.

Having Fun

Being centered and having balance is actually the opposite of pressure. Olympic swimmer Michael Phelps explained that following some disappointing performances, he worked on his balance and went from "being uptight" to "having fun in there." The techniques necessary for relaxing into your game and having fun include visualization, mental imagery, breathing, self-talk, and meditation.

Meditation

Psychologist Mihaly Csikszentmihalyi has explained the state of flow – a place of extremely high energy and focus experienced by many athletes during success. Athletes report that in this flow state, they lose the sense of the self and of time.

Meditation has been credited as one of the most effective techniques to become relaxed, focused, in balance, and in the zone. The techniques of meditation help the mind ignore distractions. Therefore, your energy, focus, and resources can be applied to the task at hand.

Meditation is often used by athletes on competition days. It helps an athlete control composure, find balance, and recharge. One study showed that runners who meditated 20 minutes a day during a six-week program had a significant improvement in their sprinting.

The head chatter is always there. It cannot necessarily be turned off, but it can be manipulated into positive, performance-enhancing techniques. Top coaches and sports psychologists say that instead of trying to lose it, *use it.* Use visualization and positive self-talk to get focused, get centered, and get ahead!

CHAPTER 9

LEAPING THE HURDLES OF YOUR MIND'S OBSTACLE COURSE

Football coach John Madden once said, "The road to easy street goes through the sewer." While this may not sound all that attractive, the truth is, before you can achieve success through passionately enjoying your sport with excellence, you do need to leap some mental hurdles. And while that may not be an obstacle course that entails literally slogging through the sewers, at times it may feel like it. The best athlete recognizes the need to "get out of your own way" and develops a mindset that leads to putting in the necessary hard work, even if it stinks.

From the Projects to the Pros (I Did It My Way)

During the season throughout my NFL career, I would train individually outside of the team's training program. This was intentional. I'd get up at 5:30 in the morning and go to the gym before heading to the stadium. The point of this was to take responsibility for my own actions. What better way for me to do this than away from the team setting. It was twofold for me. For one, even though there were eleven guys on the field and we worked together as a team, I had to perform at my peak as an individual to be able to contribute to the team.

Working out by myself with weights and running helped me not to rely on other individuals. Second, I didn't want others to know "what was in my right hand." For example, our day usually consisted of meetings at the stadium, then lunch, practice, and then we did some running. When we finished, we usually worked out in the weight room. So at that particular time, I just needed to do what was required. Some coaches couldn't figure out how I had the strength I had and just figured I was naturally strong, but that was another game. This (in my concussed mind) gave me another edge.

OBSESSIVE AND UNPRODUCTIVE CHATTER

Obsessing Over Details

A recent study by neuroscientists discovered that focused thinking about failure can affect and reduce brain activity, both sensory and motor skill directed, which in turn adversely affects the biomechanics of performance. Sports therapists explain these results by simplifying the concept: "If you think you're going to lose before you've even begun, you make it so."

Obsessing Over Winning

Sports therapists and many coaches agree that focusing on performance, rather than winning, can be more effective for successfully achieving goals. An extreme focus on winning, an obsession with winning, can put pressures on an athlete that inhibit the most effective performance.

Champion coaches are known to promote the process over results, yet their winning percentage is often undeniable. Coaches like Nick Saban and Bud Grant place emphasis on discipline and excellence for each player. John Wooden communicates to his players about his Pyramid of Success. Many coaches would agree that you don't win a championship by obsessing over the idea that "we're going to win a championship," but by looking at ways to continuously get better.

Distractions

Keeping a positive, effective focus is essential for top performance. Distractions can occur before, during, or after a performance. And yes, it's normal to have a momentary lapse in concentration, but the optimal course brings you back quickly so you can reconnect with what you aim to focus on. According to sports professionals, distraction control is one of the most important mental strengths that makes or breaks high-level performances. Sports therapists, coaches, and athletes themselves attest to the value of refocusing through the use of key words, mantras, imaging, and other reminders when distraction occurs.

The Chatter that Takes You Away from the Moment

Rumination is a word with two meanings. To ruminate is to chew repeatedly for a long time, the way livestock chew their cud. The other definition of ruminate means to go over something in the mind again and again. Consider how we ask somebody who seems upset, "What's eating you?" Well, ruminating is the act of having an attuned focus on events from the past, or dwelling on what might happen in the future, and these thoughts can eat away at your confidence. They are often negative thoughts, worries, fears, anxieties, discouragements, or a lack of forgiveness for past mistakes. All this negative head chatter causes stress right now. It prevents you from enjoying your present moment, and you get stuck in the past or the future instead of being where you should be – in the now. Being in the now is the opposite of rumination. Being in the now means focusing on what you are doing so that you have all your abilities working optimally.

If your obstacle is being stuck in a bunch of obsessive or unproductive head chatter that takes you away from your focus at hand, there are steps you can take to work on clearing your mind to focus on the present moment. For concentration, many athletes use focal points successfully, finding a focal point where you can lock your concentration, in the "on" position. Others use music that keeps them confident and calm.

Mindfulness for the Present Moment

Mindfulness teaches us to be masters of our own minds instead of letting our minds master us. Mindfulness is the opposite of being absent-minded. Many athletes find themselves less effective in their sports performances because their minds wander and they start thinking ahead, or they start falling behind into past memories rather than being fully present and tuned in to what they are currently doing.

Mindfulness is paying purposeful attention to the present moment by ignoring distracting thoughts and feelings that attempt to break your concentration on the here and now. Mindfulness techniques teach you ways to be able to keep all your energy invested in your present moment, rather than having any of it get wasted on trying to get rid of or blocking unwanted thoughts.

According to recent research, mindfulness goes to work and enhances an athlete's performance through the athlete just accepting that these wandering thoughts are there. Mindfulness is simply accepting the wandering thoughts along with responding to athletic cues and pursuing achievement goals. In this research, thinking about a bad performance or another negative thought is simply noted, accepted as a thought, and then the athlete can quickly refocus on his or her performance and goals.

Other researchers in mindfulness and athletics believe that use of mindfulness results in improvements in both an athlete's mental and physical performance. In one study on mindfulness and long-distance runners, archers, and golfers, all the subjects reported an increase in their abilities to act with awareness after a year-long program. Additionally, the runners reported improved mile times.

Mindfulness and Flow State or Zone

Recently, researchers have explained that mindfulness in athletics has similar effects to the flow or zone state where the athlete is totally absorbed in the actions and experiences at hand using both the mind and body. The researchers believe that practicing mindfulness in athletics could therefore result in an increased optimal performance.

One study on mindfulness and flow studied a group of elite golfers who completed a mindfulness training program, compared to another group who did not. All participants in the mindfulness program achieved their competition goals, moved up in their rankings, and felt an increase in their confidence using the mindfulness techniques. In the control group, only two golfers showed improvements in goals or rankings.

Continuing studies on mindfulness and performance have shown that mindfulness techniques can be a valuable mental tool that athletes can use to generally overcome or block unwanted thoughts or feelings that interfere in games or competitions.

How to Use Mindfulness

Sports therapists often recommend a body scan technique as an introductory tool for learning to use mindfulness. Sit in a comfortable chair and note each part of the body, from head, to shoulders, arms, hands, legs, feet, and how each part feels while you are resting in the chair. The way this helps is to bring your mind into focus if it drifts away due to head chatter.

Another method in mindfulness would apply to sitting comfortably and just noticing your thoughts as each one comes to your mind. But rather than worry over the thought, just give it a simple label and move on. This method is said to work with sports; for example, if a golfer worries about a swing just before he takes it, can just observe the thought and label it a "worry thought". The explanation is that putting the worry in its place with a simple description can leave the golfer free to focus on his swing at the moment.

Meditation to Put Roadblocks at Ease

Meditation has been shown in countless studies to reduce stress and improve focus, so it's no wonder more and more athletes have been using meditation to ease the anxieties that can cause missed shots, injuries, lapses in confidence, the anxiety of pressure performances, and many other peak performance blockers.

More recently, athletes in the news have revealed their positive use of meditation to benefit their sport. Teams as well have been using mindfulness and visualization practices including some meditation techniques.

All Star Kobe Bryant had told Conan O'Brien that he meditated with the team before big games.

George Mumford, a sports psychologist and meditation teacher, has worked with the Chicago Bulls and Michael Jordan on sharpening focus through meditation. Mumford said in an interview, "When we are in the moment and absorbed with the activity, we play our best. That happens once in a while, but it happens more often if we learn how to be more mindful."

Sports psychologist Michael Gervais helped Olympic volleyball gold medalists Misty May-Treanor and Kerri Walsh-Jenkins deal with pressure to stay mentally sharp using meditation, yoga. and visualization.

Former Miami Dolphins running back Ricky Williams described using daily meditation before games to counteract stress. He said, "I think a lot of people are so used to being stressed, they don't realize they're stressed. And I was one of those people."

Other sports therapists attest that many athletes use meditation to be able to relax and see themselves in positive situations.

In an interview, legendary coach Phil Jackson revealed the meditative ideas behind his coaching methods. "One breath, one mind," Jackson said, "I approached it with mindfulness. As much as we pump iron and we run to build our strength up, we need to build our mental strength up. So we can focus, so we can be in concert with one another."

Fear of Failure or Losing

"If you can't accept losing, you can't win." So said football coach Vince Lombardi.

Golfer Greg Norman said, "I never feared anything or anyone on the course and I wasn't afraid to fail. So I think I'd do pretty well against Snead, Hogan, Tiger and Phil – whoever."

"If you trust your nerve as well as your skill, you're capable of a lot more than you can imagine," said Olympic skater Debi Thomas.

Losing is not pleasant. Nobody likes to lose. It's frustrating, demoralizing, a blow. Many athletes are afraid to make a mistake or to fail, feeling it is the worst thing in the world. The job is to see what went wrong and what can be done differently. Sports therapists, coaches, and other athletes all agree that to go the limits in sports, it takes risks, putting it all on the line, going for it, and understanding that there will be many times of coming up short and falling flat. It's all normal. But all the professionals agree, without failure, there can never be success. It's never a measure of inadequacy and it is never a reason to beat yourself up.

One coach offered a motivating phrase to address losing or failure: "Be curious, not furious."

Having and Maintaining Personal Trust

Coaches and psychologists agree that athletes can't really know what their limits are because there is always the potential level of "better than you think" or "better than your best." But it is only when an athlete can relax and trust in himself or herself to have worked the best – to have taken the best training, to relax, to allow a peak performance, to let flow take over – can he or she get to those levels.

Trust comes from putting in hard, daily, consistent training. Trusting counteracts the roadblocks of ruminating or focusing too much on past mistakes. Trust leads to being able to let go of mistakes and refocus.

Some sports professionals have recommended making a mental mistake folder that can be taken out to work on at the proper time and place.

General Obstacles to Thinking

There are some thoughts that are not helpful, thoughts that are obstacles to progress and athletic achievement and performance. Here are some pointers to counteract general attitudes that can be real mental roadblocks in athletics.

1. Keep your thinking positive. Don't let negative thinking – either yours or other people's – run away with your mind. There's always something to be grateful for and always something positive to focus on. If you have a setback or frustrations in accomplishing a goal, it won't always be that way. Keep your path in mind as a path you develop yourself, rather than seeing a present setback as the destination itself.

2. Take it easy and refrain from expectations that things will be easy. Sports therapists, coaches, and other athletes attest that facing challenges is what makes you strong, and facing continuing challenges is what it takes to be successful by building up your knowledge, strength, and abilities.

3. Learn to be master of your head chatter so that you're never a prisoner of past mistakes or failures by going back to them at inopportune times. Don't let self-confidence slip. If you have failures, it's OK to start over in a different way.

Accepting Weaknesses for Building Strength

Reviewing any and all weakness in a performance is essential to growing and learning how to do it better. Recognize what skills or moves need to be improved and focus on them in practice. This type of reflection should not be a roadblock. It shouldn't affect your self-confidence or motivation, but it's a positive challenge to refine your mental readiness and focus.

Olympic canoeing champion Larry Cain reported, "It has become more important to identify as closely as possible where I've screwed up, and then to work on that in practice to make sure it doesn't happen again. By analyzing my race stroke for stroke, figuring out what I did wrong, I can put together a more perfect race. The idea is, you try and recall exactly what happened in the race and gain from it. I'm always repeating the plan in practice and working on certain points that I can identify as screw-ups in a previous race."

Tiger Woods is known to have changed his stroke when he believed his timing was off and hurting his game. Athletes need to emulate the ways sports heroes have the guts to do that, to not be afraid of weaknesses, but to embrace them.

Peyton Manning once said, "After a loss like this, we just have to go back and work harder. We got outplayed and that's all there is to it. You have to let it go, move on, and just work harder."

Losing is not the end of the world, but a necessary part of future success. It's the opportunity to take your game to the next level. Michael Jordan is not hesitant to reveal, "I've missed more than 9,000 shots in my career. I've lost almost 300 games. Twenty-six times I have been trusted to take the game winning shot and missed. I've failed over and over again in my life, and that is why I succeed." To be sure, he has succeeded!

However, sports therapists also advise you to reflect on what you did well!

Competing Against More Skilled Opponents

Tennis champion Maria Sharapova said, "In the last year, I have gained a lot of experience because I have been playing against top players and realized what things to work on to get better. Top players basically tell you what your weaknesses are on the court."

Sports therapists and other athletes would agree with Sharapova that playing against more skilled opponents puts you in a good position to learn and develop by highlighting your weaknesses. This is, of course, not always easy to see as a favor. But keep in mind how some coaches have been known to say, "Feedback is the breakfast of champions." So focusing on weaknesses actually can propel you to be your best.

Comparing Yourself to Others

Why does comparing damage you? It's because often you will overestimate and inflate the other person's assets and gloss over or minimize their weaknesses, while simultaneously overestimating and inflating your own weaknesses and minimizing your strengths. Keep your focus on your own development. And keep in mind that it is great to have role models, people whose skills you'd like to emulate or use as inspiration.

Trying Too Hard – Self-Pressure, Forcing, and Then Choking

Pressuring oneself has been shown to tighten muscles and interfere with performance, while peak performance occurs with the opposite – being relaxed, trusting instincts, and letting it happen. Thinking too much with pressure, trying too hard, or forcing it can slow down mind and body processes and distract from the task at hand.

The ability to perform without self-pressure is about changing from being stuck inside your head during a tournament. What is optimal is to be in the zone or flow, where you are performing fully immersed, energized, focused, involved, and enjoying the process. This is what makes an optimally performed skill look effortless, because the body is doing what it is trained to do.

Brazilian soccer star Pele once said, "If you ever want to be a decent player, you have to be able to use both feet without stopping to think about it."

One sports therapist recommended this exercise to turn skills into second nature so it all feels natural:

Close your eyes and think about the number 1. If you start to notice your mind wandering to any other thought, just go to number two until your mind loses focus again, and then move on to number three, and so on.

This method helps to train the brain to be able to come right back to the task at hand.

Focusing on Uncontrollable Aspects

When an athlete focuses on things he or she can't control, either before or during a performance, it can affect attitude by causing anxiety and feeling uptight. It can damage confidence, trust, and concentration, and the chances of a peak performance are ruined. Uncontrollable things include the opponents, playing conditions, the crowd, expectations, past mistakes, and future outcomes. If an athlete finds himself or herself focusing on any of these uncontrollable aspects, he or she must learn how to return the focus to the task at hand.

Taking responsibility for Your Actions

Blaming others for failures or setbacks is a major "head hurdle" to success. Coaches and sports therapists agree that to be successful is to recognize that everything is up to you – you are responsible for the training you put in.

Overthinking

Peak performance, as Pele said, is about not thinking, it's about being on automatic, with a mind that's quiet, letting your well-trained muscle memory do what you've trained it to do. When you are performing or competing, it is not the time to be instructing and criticizing yourself. It's important to trust your muscle memory. This means you have put in the hard work in training without cutting corners, and you feel confident in your ability to do that.

A recent study revealed that right-handed athletes who squeezed a ball with their left hand were less likely to choke. Science explains this result in the belief that thinking occurs in the left side of the brain, while automated behavior occurs on the right. Each side of the brain controls the opposite side's movement. So a left hand is connected to the right side of the body, and therefore squeezing the ball with the left hand would activate the ride side of the brain, which is the automatic behavior motor skills, rather than the left brain thinking and pondering.

Pushing Out of the Comfort Zone

Being complacent in a comfort zone, rather than pushing out of it to the next level of difficulty, is a definite roadblock to improvement and peak performance.

If fear of failure is a reason for not attempting the next level, coaches recommend recognizing that fear is natural. Ross Hindman, founder of International Snowboard Training Center in Colorado and California, attests, "Everybody feels fear out there, and I mean everybody. The issue is how you deal with fear." Sports therapists use techniques of mental imagery, self-talk, and breathing to help athletes deal with the fear of training that's difficult or uncomfortable, and when they shy away from training for unknown reasons.

Freestyle skiing gold medalist Peter Olenick mastered his fear and described his self-invented whisky flip. "It was terrifying," said Peter, "I didn't even know if it could be done, but I'd been doing it over and over in my head, so I figured I could make it go right – some deep breaths, some mental finger crossing – and I just kind of did it." He admitted his second attempt was "even scarier [since] now my body knew what was happening. But I did it. Fear kind of keeps all of us going."

A published study at New York University researched a method of making a fearful memory feel safe by rewriting its emotional impact. In the study, participants were conditioned to fear a flashing blue square with a mild wrist shock. Then the flashing blue squares were repeated the next day with no shock. A subgroup was also given another exposure to the blue squares without the shock again, so that they would still have the fearful memory in mind, and when they immediately saw the blue squares without the shock, they were able to rewrite the fearful feelings and were no longer afraid of them.

The researchers of the NYU study recommended that revising memories in this manner should be done when the memory is still fresh in the mind.

The lead author of the study, Dr. Daniela Schiller, explains that in the mental process, when you call up a memory of your unpleasant vision and quickly overlay it with a pleasant vision of the same maneuver, your mind can be revised. The content isn't gone, of course, but what is changed is your emotions around it that will make the mistake, the unpleasant circumstance, or the fear now tolerable.

Peter Olenick uses this type of training to combat his fears when he watches a video of himself failing, noting his every inefficient movement, flailing, crashing, and ending up lying down. But then, he uses his mental imagery to reimagine how he will do it better the next time.

Otherwise, athletes have been known to use padding helmets, wrist guards, kneepads, butt pads – whatever is needed – to learn a new skill and keep confidence boosted.

Jeff Mugleston, manager of Snow Sports School at Taos, shares that fear is a good thing that makes you act smarter.

Remember the following inspirational quotes offered by well-known champs:

"Never let the fear of striking out get in your way." –Babe Ruth

"Of all the hazards, fear is the worst." –Sam Snead

Perfectionism

There is a difference between striving for perfection and being a perfectionist. Striving is putting in the work doing whatever you can to strengthen yourself to reach that goal of perfection. But being a perfectionist usually means a person critically judges him or herself for failing at perfection, and thus loses confidence. This may also result in an athlete choosing to make every effort not to fail, avoiding anything that might lead to failure. This can cause someone to miss out on what is necessary to learn and grow and perfect skills.

Sports therapists recommend compassion. Have compassion for yourself; don't be so hard on yourself, as they say. Give yourself a pat on the back for the good accomplishments and hard work. And sports therapists recommend laughter. A sense of humor has been studied and recognized as stress reducing, mood lifting, and positive in every may. Laugh, give yourself a break, and move on.

Burnout

Pushing too much – not taking care of the bodily needs for adequate nutrition and rest – can lead to exhaustion, injuries, and loss of energy, meaning, and focus. This is the condition of being "overcooked" and burned out. Athletes, just like everyone, need a healthy mind and a healthy body to reach goals and dreams. All of us need the proper time to recharge and to keep ourselves in balance.

The simple fact is that even professional athletes need to learn how to get out of their own way. They, like all of us, bring baggage that can block performance. Some can't get past their fear of failure; some struggle with a nagging sense of inadequacy regarding their skills; and some feel the pressure of having to score all the time or beat out the competition to be a starter.

Quieting the chatter of your mind's obstacle course means accepting who you are, all of you – your limitations, failures, the whole picture. And with this acceptance comes the viewpoint of seeing these parts of your life not as insurmountable hurdles, but a yellow brick road to your learning about your ultimate athletic success.

SECTION IV

WE ARE THE CHAMPIONS

CHAPTER 10

GREAT ATHLETES – WHAT SETS THEM APART?

The remarkable achievements of sports champions can bring us to our feet in amazement, and this makes us ask the question: could we ever come near a performance like that? Well, hopefully, in our own venues, working with our own talents, skills, and passions, each of us will go as far as we can dream.

What sets great athletes apart is that they combine their talents, skills, and passions to the nth degree and beyond, showing the world and proving to all that the beauty, splendor, and perfection of athletics is indeed humanly possible – and furthermore, that it is possible to have all of that wrapped up in a single individual. The next one could be you.

Here is a selection of five athletes we particularly admire as champions for all time.

Bruce Lee

In just 33 years, Bruce Lee singularly accomplished what would normally take several talented people to offer the world.

It is not easy to separate the components of Bruce Lee's athleticism, since his many facets, including his abilities, skills, leadership, thinking, and performance are all essential parts of who he was as a champion.

Considered by critics and the media to be one of the most influential martial artists of all time, Lee is loved and admired across the generations as a pop culture icon – an action film actor, a martial artist, a filmmaker, and a philosopher.

Lee was not just an athlete of marital arts prowess, he influenced the whole realm and direction of martial arts in his native Hong Kong and throughout the entire world.

Lee initially trained in Wing Chun and boxing. During his lifetime, the martial art style was strict and well defined. His passion and motivation to go further in the arts was what drove him to develop his own martial arts philosophy, using a variety of existent sources and innovative techniques.

Lee had a huge, powerful, fiery presence. Fittingly enough, he was born in the Chinese year and hour of the dragon. Growing up, Bruce lived in a neighborhood filled with drugs and gang rivalries. As a teen, he was a street fighter. A police detective warned Lee's father that his son had been fighting in school and if his fighting continued, he would be in danger of going to jail. It was due to his involvement in street fights that he began learning martial arts. After the police officer's warning, Lee elected to work on his training privately. He had the mental and emotional strength to learn from his mistakes, make changes, look into himself, and become a teacher and leader of the martial arts in Seattle.

From there, Bruce Lee was never satisfied with his development and exploration of the martial arts. At two Long Beach International Karate Championships, he used two-finger push-ups, a one-hand punch, and performed what became a famous unstoppable punch.

While becoming a film star in "The Green Hornet," Lee was inspired by the techniques of his fighting role. He was critical of them, but Lee was always looking for ways to improve on them. He developed a system of practicality, flexibility, speed, and efficiency. In his training, Lee used a combination of weight training for strength, running for endurance, and stretching for flexibility. While designing his training regimen, Lee developed a technique that blended his earlier techniques derived from fencing, boxing, judo, and Kung Fu. He called this system "Jeet Kune Do" – the Way of the Intercepted Fist.

Bruce Lee did not *magically* develop his athletic, physical, mental, and emotional skills, but was instead dedicated to his fitness routines. He always had a goal of being as strong as he could possibly be. Lee's philosophy in athletics promoted not just skills, but also attitude. He believed that too much time was spent on skill development, while development of the spirit was just as necessary.

Lee was seriously devoted to nutrition and health foods, high-protein drinks, and vitamin supplements. He proclaimed that junk foods and the wrong kind of fuel for the body could not lead to achievement of a high-performance body.

Bruce Lee was certainly a champion. He filled the role's definition with passion, mental toughness, confidence, courage, commitment, positive thinking, and a strong belief in himself. He achieved unstoppable growth through personal development and a moral, humble character. Lee was a dedicated inspirational leader and teacher and a true continuous learner.

Lee inspired many cultural changes, such as leading the way toward a more fluid, realistic approach to martial arts and combat in movie making by using dance techniques (he was reported to be a champion cha-cha dancer).

Bruce Lee was just a regular guy who, when pushed, become like an army and inspired others to do the same. Lee empowered people of multiple ethnicities. His diverse popularity played a major role in promoting the transformation of cross-cultural attitudes about racial equality, harmony, and acceptance. He changed the goals of those who work out at gyms from "beefing up" to goals of power, speed, and looking and feeling good.

So much of what sports psychologists and coaches have advised and taught in recent years, as well as the techniques that are described and discussed throughout this book, resonate in the following quotes by Bruce Lee:

- "A goal is not always meant to be reached, it often serves simply as something to aim at."

- "If you spend too much time thinking about a thing, you'll never get it done. Make at least one definite move daily toward your goal."

- "Ever since I was a child, I have had this instinctive urge for expansion and growth. To me, the function and duty of a quality human being is the sincere and honest development of one's potential"

- "I am not teaching you anything, I just help you to explore yourself."

- "Life itself is your teacher, and you are in a state of constant learning."

- "Mistakes are always forgivable if one has the courage to admit them."

- "The great mistake is to anticipate the outcome of the engagement. You ought not be thinking of whether it ends in victory or defeat. Let nature take its course and your tools will strike at the right moment."

- "Choose the positive. You have choice, you are master of your attitude. Choose the positive, the constructive. Optimism is a faith that leads to success."

- "If you think a thing is impossible, you'll make it impossible."

- "To hell with circumstances; I create opportunities."

- "I am learning to understand rather than to immediately judge or be judged."

- "I am happy because I am growing daily, and I am honestly not knowing where the limit lies. To be certain, every day there can be a revelation or a new discovery. I treasure the memory of the past misfortunes. It has added more to my bank of fortitude."

- "Do not be tense; just be ready, not thinking, not dreaming, not being set, but being flexible. It is being wholly and quietly alive, aware, and alert, ready for whatever may come."

- "I fear not the man who has practiced 10,000 kicks once, but I fear the man who has practiced one kick 10,000 times."

- "One should be in harmony with, not in opposition to, the strength and force of the opposition. The important thing is not to strain in any way."

- "Fear comes from uncertainty; we can eliminate the fear within us when we know ourselves better."

"The biggest adversary in our life is ourselves. We are what we are, in a sense, because of the dominating thoughts we allow to gather in our head. A great deal of pure self-knowledge and inner understanding allows us to lay an all-important foundation for the structure of our life from which we can perceive and take the right avenues. To become different from what we are, we must have some awareness of what we are. To know oneself is to study oneself in action with another person."

- "Flow in the living moment. We are always in a process of becoming, and nothing is fixed. Moving, be like water. Still be like a mirror. Respond like an echo."

- "Awareness is without choice, without demand, without anxiety; in that state of mind, there is perception."

- "Take no thought of who is right or wrong or who is better than. Be not for or against."

- "What is more important than what should be? Too many people are looking at what is from a position of thinking what should be."

Given that Lee lived from 1940-1973, and the practice of sport psychology only become relevant at the Olympic games in 1984, Bruce Lee was way ahead of his time.

Wilma Rudolph

Wilma Rudolph reminds one of a rocket ship blasting off with speed and power, blazing a new trail into the universe, and then falling back to earth, her name and path traced and known and affecting many, as she is forever remembered in historical records.

Wilma Rudolph will always be remembered as a champion who overcame countless obstacles throughout her entire life. Despite all odds, with her harmonious passion, will, deep-seated conviction, and belief in herself, Rudolph became a three-time Olympic gold medal winner in track with records that made her the fastest woman in track and field.

Wilma Rudolph was born and raised in a small town in Tennessee, the 20th child of 22 children. She was born prematurely during an era characterized with discrimination and societal limits set for black women. In her childhood, she endured double pneumonia, scarlet fever, whooping cough, measles, chicken pox, and worst of all, polio at age four. Due to the medical science of the time, Rudolph was told that she would never walk. Despite being unable to afford good medical care, her family is a shining example of the wonders that valuable support can do for a person, and their support was an essential part of Wilma's success. The support was never financial, but Rudolph's mother took her on long bus trips every week for therapy sessions, and her siblings massaged her legs four times a day. As Rudolph wrote in her autobiography, "My father pushed me to become competitive. He felt that sports would help me overcome the problems." Whether it was the massages, the therapy sessions, or simply Wilma's indomitable will, at age eight she was able to walk with a leg brace. When asked about her leg braces, Rudolph said, "I spent most of my time trying to figure out how to get them off, but when you come from a large wonderful family, there's always a way to achieve your goals." By age 12, Rudolph was able to play basketball barefoot, without any support.

At 13, just nine years after her prognosis, Rudolph made the all-state basketball team, and she would occasionally skip school to run on a track. While playing on her high school basketball team in 10th grade, she was spotted by Tennessee State track and field coach Ed Temple, who encouraged her to run. Rudolph showed an incredible drive, making it her mission to participate in Temple's daily college practice.

Her talent, positive focus, and energy was evident in all that she did. It glowed through her performances. Rudolph ran her way into the 1956 Olympics while still in high school, winning a bronze medal in the women's 400-meter relay. At the 1960 Olympics, she won three gold medals for the 100-meter, the 200-meter, and the 400-meter relays — and she won these medals despite a sprained ankle! Rudolph broke records, and she became the fastest woman in the world.

Wilma Rudolph was the first female American Olympic champion who was seen on television, but it is her spirit reflected in her words that is truly remarkable.

"I came out second or third in the field, and my speed started increasing the farther I went. When I reached 50 meters, I saw that I had them all and I was just beginning to turn it on. By 70 meters, I knew the race was mine, nobody was going to catch me."

Rudolph is a shining example of a champion athlete whose whole life was devoted to her goals, not solely her sports. Many would say that she had the greatest impact on issues of gender roles in athletics; she changed the norm in her lifetime and inspired women in track. She helped elevate women's track to a major establishment in the world of sports. Rudolph believed that she had a greater purpose in life than just medals and sports acclaim, and she was involved in many humanitarian endeavors and projects: she founded the Wilma Rudolph Foundation to help children with discipline, work, and sports, a feat that she believed to be her greatest accomplishment. Rudolph earned a teaching degree and became a teacher and a track coach at DePauw University. She was a goodwill ambassador to West Africa and a devoted mother of four children. Rudolph is recognized as a major supporter of the African-American community, and she was an important civil rights and women's rights pioneer. At a Homecoming parade and banquet following an American Olympic team tour, Rudolph assured the crowd that this was an integrated event, the first fully integrated municipal event in her city's history.

Wilma Rudolph was named Associated Press Female Athlete of the Year in both 1960 and 1961. She was inducted into the U.S. Olympic Hall of Fame and the National Women's Hall of Fame, but all of these honors don't adequately encompass the calm and grace for which people remember her, or her memorable words of determination, will, and spirituality:

- "I tell them the most important aspect is to be yourself and have confidence in yourself. I remind them the triumph can't be had without the struggle."

- "Winning is great, sure, but if you are really going to do something in life, the secret is learning how to lose. Nobody goes undefeated all the time. If you can pick up after a crushing defeat, and go on to win again, you are going to be a champion someday."

- "I ran and ran and ran every day, and I acquired this sense of determination, this sense of spirit that I would never, never give up, no matter what else happened."

- "It doesn't matter what you're trying to accomplish. It's all a matter of discipline."

Wilma Rudolph died of a brain tumor at the young age of 54. As Jackie Joyner-Kersee said, "She laid the foundation for all of us women who wanted to aspire to be great athletes."

Dan Gable

Dan Gable, an American wrestler and coach, is known as a winner with unprecedented record success, a staggering succession of wins, and an ability to bring it all home with his mental toughness, intensity, discipline, and perseverance It is a monumental task to find words to describe Gable's earned fame as a champion.

As head coach of Iowa's wrestling team, Gable is still talked about for his record dynasty. From 1978 to 1986, Gable led the Hawkeyes to unbelievable success, winning the NCAA title nine years in a row. He led the Hawkeyes to 25 consecutive Big Ten championships and 16 national titles. His coaching record had a winning percentage of .938.

Before Dan Gable became a highly-acclaimed coach, he was a high-performance athlete himself. Gable was an Olympic wrestler who won a gold medal without giving up a single point. He was an athlete of fierce concentration, attention, and focus, the kind of focus that drove his successful wrestling and coaching career.

During his high school and college years, Gable compiled an amazing 181-1 record. He showed his tenacity and mental toughness early in his career, and he used his only loss to rebound and win the Olympic gold medal. Gable is quoted as saying, "I vowed I wouldn't ever let anyone destroy me again. I was going to work at it every day, so hard that I would be the toughest guy in the world. By the end of practice, I wanted to be physically tired, to know that I'd been through a workout. If I wasn't tired, I must have cheated somehow, so I stayed a little longer."

Gable believes that his absolute focus on wrestling began immediately following his sister's tragic murder. He used his emotions as fuel to relentlessly master his techniques. Even after his single loss, which Gable admitted left him in tears, he picked himself up, ready to do not just his best, but even better. Just two weeks later, Gable followed that single loss with winning the National AAUs, where he received the award of Outstanding Wrestler. Gable reveals an important quality about athletics in respect to losing and learning from mistakes: "I needed to get beat because it not just helped me win the Olympics, but it helped me dominate the Olympics. But more than that, it helped me be a better coach. I would have a hundred times rather not have that happened, but I used it."

Gable's luminous coaching career was not limited anywhere. Along with his prolific nine-year national championship streak with the Hawkeyes, Gable was also the coach of the Olympic freestyle team and guided them to seven gold medals in one year.

Gable would have used his aggressive spirit to coach wrestling for his entire life, but more than twelve knee and back surgeries left him with no choice but to retire from coaching. But even this wasn't the end of Dan Gable. The physical limitations that prevented him from getting down on the mat to demonstrate moves did not get prevent him from using his passion and knowledge to teach others. To this day, Dan Gable continues to keep himself close to the sport that has been his life.

Always working to promote the benefits of wrestling, Gable has hosted a series of instructional DVDs. According to Gable, "I don't care what kind of job you have, you still have to pay attention to detail to be exceptional. And that usually takes a lot of discipline. Ours is one sport where you have to be disciplined in several ways, and you don't get to take any shortcuts."

He maintains the same grit that he carried throughout his wrestling and coaching years. Gable recently revealed in an interview, "I never wore a mouthpiece." When asked why, gable explained that it would have made him feel weak and vulnerable, and his method was to welcome pain, to harden his face and his muscles. "It makes you strong," Gable professes.

As powerful and fearsome as he was with his sport, Dan Gable has always been a family man. "My wrestling and family go together. It's always been that way from day one with my mom, my dad, my sister, my wife, four daughters, grandsons, and sons-in-law. They're all here." His family has always supported his career, and he has always prioritized paying attention to them, never choosing career over family.

One of Gable's most successful training methods, the method he used to gain his seemingly superhuman stamina and resiliency, is the method of recovery. He explains that his commitment to a recovery routine after every practice was equally as important, if not more so, than the intense way in which he trained. Gable's recovery routine includes stretching, sauna, steam, massage, and mental relaxation. For him, recovery is a time to analyze the day's events, both good and bad. It is a time spend analyzing his actions and the different ways that he responded both physically, mentally, and emotionally. Using these reflections, Gable develops a plan for the next day's course of action.

Dan Gable's mettle, intensity, and mental toughness is evident in his words:

- "Gold medals aren't really made of gold. They're made of sweat, determination, and a hard-to-find alloy called guts."

- "No one ever drowned in sweat."

- "If you're afraid to fail, you'll never succeed."

- "When I lifted weights, I didn't lift just to maintain my muscle tone. I lifted to increase what I already had, to push to a new limit. Every time I worked out, I was getting a little better. I kept moving that limit back and back. Every time I walked out of the gym, I was a little better than when I walked in."

- "More enduringly than any other sport, wrestling teaches self-control and pride. Some have wrestled without great skill – none have wrestled without pride."

Dan Gable's career as an athlete and coach can be summed up fairly simply: his unsurpassed ability allowed him to bring out the very best in himself and in others. Today, Gable is a renowned motivational speaker on the topics of overcoming adversity, team building, and achieving peak performance in everything you do.

Nadia Comaneci

Courage, commitment, balance, determination, focus, confidence, character, and most of all, perfection.

There are many adjectives and accolades that are used to describe champion athletes, but perfect is a rare one – and Nadia Comaneci, who was a perfect 10 Olympic champion, is truly a rare athlete.

With her characteristic humility, she humbly recalls her goal-oriented technique, at work through her competition process. "First of all, it was not '10,' it was a one point zero because the computers couldn't cope. ... It's hard to believe it's 36 years since I did that, it doesn't feel that long, but it is. I remember everything, all the routines." Fittingly enough, Comaneci does not proffer an opinion on what perfection is. "There is no definition of perfection. At some particular time when I was 14 years old," Comaneci said, "I've done something that people didn't expect. It's a ladder that you climb in life, and I got there first."

Nadia Comaneci began her athletic life with strong commitment and a passionate goal. "Olga Korbut was the famous gymnast at that time, but I was watching her in the gymnastics and I said to myself, I hope one day I will be like her." And sure enough, Nadia became even more.

She began learning gymnastics at the young age of six, and although at first she didn't know she wanted to be a gymnast, she quickly recognized her love of competition, saying, "Probably if I didn't do gymnastics I would have done a different sport, and hopefully I would have been good enough."

While Comaneci would have likely succeeded in any sport she chose, the entire world took notice of the young Olympian's athleticism and grace. Comaneci has become an inspiration and role model to a generation of gymnasts. She holds strong to the belief that what is most important is every person's own unique development, rather than thinking that young gymnasts should emulate her. As Comaneci commented, "I don't think you should replicate what I've done – everybody has to be unique. I think kids should have role models, but I don't think you should duplicate anybody. You should create your own thing."

Comaneci spent many hours of training from an early age on. She would train six to seven hours a day in order to reach a level of optimal performance. Comaneci explains that her dedication to training and her mental toughness have ultimately been the key aspects of her success. "You have to have a lot passion for what you do to be able to work hard and to have a lot of motivation, because you're going to go to places that you're never going to believe. I don't run away from a challenge because I am afraid. Instead, I run toward it because the only way to escape fear is to trample it beneath your foot. ... Hard work has made it easy. That is my secret. That is why I win. ... I don't do many things. But if I do one, I do it well. I don't give half."

When Nadia was eight, she came in 13th at the National Rome Championships, and just one year later, she took first. She was the youngest winner on record.

At age 13, she became an all-around gold medal winner in the European Championships in Norway, and she continued to win. The following year, she acquired a perfect 10 at Madison Square Garden as well as 10s in other meets, proving to the world that her perfection wasn't just luck, but the product of hard work and dedication.

Nadia Comaneci is a two-time recipient of the highest award given by the International Olympic Committee, the Olympic Order. she was inducted in the International Gymnastics Hall of Fame, and she won five Olympic Gold Medals.

Nadia Comaneci has maintained a positive outlook, always showing respect and caring for others. Recently, she served on the International Board of Directors for the Special Olympics. Comaneci is on the Board for the Muscular Dystrophy Association, as well as founding the Nadia Comaneci Clinic.

Looking more closely at Comaneci's techniques that earned her outstanding scores reveals that she developed clean technique as well as difficult and creative skills. She was the first gymnast to perform an aerial walkover and aerial cartwheel-back handspring flight series, as well as being the first to perform a double twist dismount.

Through reading Nadia Comaneci's words of advice to young people, one gains a true understanding of her solid core values.

- "I like to tell young people to work hard for your goals and live in the moment. You should also appreciate the goodness around you, and surround yourself with positive people."

- "My definition of success is reaching or trying my best to reach a goal. Being able to do something that you want to do or should do may be hard when you do not have any support around you, so I think that having friends and family members to support you is also a part of success. "

- "It is important to have a specific goal before you even try to reach it, or else it would be very hard to know what you really want to do. ... It is important to have the ability to let go of the mistakes that you have made in the past because this is what drags you back from reaching success."

Michael Jordan

Young or old, sports enthusiast or otherwise, everyone knows of Michael Jordan. His genuineness, sincerity, and approachability have been popularized by media, but his abilities and unsurpassable success are the backbone of being the admirable champion he is.

It's easy to feel you know Michael Jordan. He's a hero – maybe even a superhero – and certainly a role model and a superstar. But most impressively, Jordan didn't need one ounce of media attention to achieve his success.

As a role model for children, he speaks of the necessary elements to become a champion, not just in sports, but in anything at all. People of all ages find Jordan immediately worth emulating.

"My appetite to learn was born out of my desire to eventually have as much control over the process as possible. Even at the end of my career, I was always comparing myself to other players. I always wanted to be sure I was doing everything I could to stay on top. I never thought a role model should be negative."

Michael Jordan makes himself available to the Make-A-Wish Foundation and greets children with cheer who approach him. He is reported to put them at ease through making them laugh, and his humility makes it possible for them to have some basketball enjoyment and not feel pressured to be around arguably the most skilled player to have ever picked up a basketball.

Michael Jordan's accomplishments are so vast that when it comes to skills, numbers, wins, honors, and awards, it is impossible to list all of them. Among his many accomplishments, Jordan has won two Olympic gold medals, six NBA championships, numerous top-scoring titles, four league MVPs, and the highest career score average of all time. Jordan has been named the greatest basketball player of all time by the National Basketball Association. He was on the cover of Sports Illustrated one month after beginning with the Chicago Bulls. The headline read, "A Star is Born." And Jordan has been called Mr. Clutch due to his many game winning shots.

Jordan is the perfect all-around basketball player, notable in both offense and defense. He was elected to the NBA's all-defensive first team in nearly every season that he played. Jordan has led the league in steals many times. He has been named the greatest point guard ever, the greatest shooting guard to ever play the game, the greatest small forward to ever set foot on a basketball court, and a top power forward and center.

Michael Jordan's dedication, determination, and commitment have made him the most successful basketball player of all time. He possesses a "never give up" attitude, which always shines. Jordan played when he was hurt countless times, and even led the Bulls to the playoffs (and had a 63-point performance) all with a broken foot! His record of going year after year without winning in the playoffs to finally winning a world championship is the ultimate example of the adage, "If at first you don't succeed…"

When it comes to core values, Jordan's are especially admirable, especially in our world today! According to Jordan, "My mother is my root, my foundation. She planted the seed that I base my life on, and that is the belief that the ability to achieve starts in your mind. The minute you get away from fundamentals – whether it's proper technique, work ethic, or mental preparation – the bottom can fall out of your game, your schoolwork, your job, whatever you're doing."

Jordan inspires us with the will to excel because he makes it seem easy, an art that just comes from within. However, he will always attest to the work that must go into any performance, and how necessary it is to possess the ability required to accept failure and losses.

- "I've missed more than 9,000 shots in my career. I've lost almost 300 games. Twenty-six times, I've been trusted to take the game winning shot and missed. I've failed over and over and over again in my life. And that is why I succeed."

- "If you push me toward something that you think is a weakness, then I will turn that perceived weakness into a strength."

- "If you run into a wall, don't turn around and give up. Figure out how to climb it, go through it, or work around it."

- "If you quit once, it becomes a habit. Never quit."

- "Never say never, because limits, like fears, are often just an illusion."

Michael Jordan, with all his fame and plentiful fortune, remains honorable, dignified, respected, and well-adjusted. He is truly a one-of-a-kind champion, and it is no wonder so many want to be "like Mike," like a true high-performance champion in his sport.

CONCLUSION

So, there you have it – everything you need to take your mind game to the next level.

Whether you're an athlete, trainer, or coach, we hope we have provided you with valuable information you can use to become – or create – a champion.

We've given you the tools to ignite your passion and create a highlight reel in your head. You've learned about the three "C's" of Confidence, Courage, and Commitment, and how to train your brain for peak performance.

After reading *Mind Over Head Chatter*, you'll know how to "get centered," visualize, and relax as you perform at YOUR highest level.

Now, all you have to do is take the first step in your journey to success!

REFERENCE

(Mind Over Head Chatter: The Psychology of Athletic Success)

http://www.entrepreneur.com/article/219709#ixzz2k5OVeKY9

http://blog.drstankovich.com/the-importance-of-passion-purpose-for-sport-success/many athletes

http://www.er.uqam.ca/nobel/r26710/LRCS/papers/vallerand_mageau2008.pdf

https://www.competitivedge.com/burnout

http://www.thesportinmind.com/.../positive-psychology-for-peak-performance

http://www.scielo.cl/scielo.php?pid=S0718-48082013000100004

http://www.scielo.cl/scielo.php?pid=S0718-8082013000100004&script=sci_arttext

https://etd.ohiolink.edu/ap:0:0:APPLICATION_PROCESS=DOWNLOAD_ETD_SUB_DOC_ACCNUM:::F1501_ID:miami1312937508,attachmenthttps://etd.ohiolink.edu/ap:0:0:APPLICATION_PROCESS=DOWNLOAD_ETD_SUB_DOC_ACCNUM:::F1501_ID:miami1312937508,attachment

http://www.abc.net.au

www.thesun.co.uk

http://www.sciencedaily.com

http://au.christiantoday.com/article/science-shows-how-passion-for-sport-keeps-you-going/14982.htm

http://www.philstar.com/sports/2013/11/07/1253964/olympic-winner-runners-pursue-your-passion-chase-your-dream

http://blog.bufferapp.com/the-myth-of-passion-and-motivation-how-to-stay-focused-when-you-get-bored-working-toward-your-goals

http://rosstraining.com/blog/2012/11/20/passion-as-a-trainer

http://www.pickthebrain.com/blog/passion/

http://www.cbsnews.com/8301-504763_162-20008153-10391704.html

http://www.arichall.com/academic/papers/psy8840-sport-psyc.pdf

http://keepingscore.blogs.time.com/2013/11/12/miami-dolphins-owner-on-bullying-scandal-this-is-so-appalling/#ixzz2kUUD57Oz

http://sportsmedicine.about.com/od/sportspsychology/qt/Support-Confidence.htm

http://www.athleteassessments.com/articles/success_of_coach_athlete_relationships.html

http://www.athleticinsight.com/Vol3Iss2/SupportPDF.pdf

http://blogs.culture.gov.uk/main/2010/12/supporting_elite_athletes_is_k.html

http://www.olympic.org/content/olympic-athletes/athletes-space/entourage-intro/

http://www.jssm.org/vol2/n1/1/v2n1-1pdf.pdf

http://www.freepatentsonline.com/article/North-American-Journal-Psychology/281111806.html

http://hpsnz.org.nz/about-us/our-expertise/athlete-performance-support

http://www.teamsynergysports.com/ATHLETES_ONLY.html

http://usafootball.com/blogs/americas-game/post/7377#sthash.ES4AEFkk. dpuf

http://www.styleweekly.com/richmond/train-your-brain/ Content?oid=1640797

http://www.facebook.com/GeorgeStuddFT

http://www.exceednutrition.com/uncategorized/6-steps-to-a-positive-successful-mindset/#sthash.ixz7vrOj.dpuf

http://www.exceednutrition.com/uncategorized/6-steps-to-a-positive-successful-mindset/

www.letssandbox.com

http://www.bobbielaporte.com/article-highlight-reel.pdf

http://www.americanathletemag.com/ArticleView/tabid/156/ArticleID/201/A-Special-Forces-Focus-All-in-Your-Head.aspx#sthash.XjhIx2C2.dpuf

http://www.americanathletemag.com/ArticleView/tabid/156/ArticleID/201/A-Special-Forces-Focus-All-in-Your-Head.aspx

http://www.mindseyesports.com/the-gym-that-never-closes/

http://www.menshealth.co.uk/fitness/sports-training/brad-picketts-ufc-blog-psychological-preparation

http://blog.teamsnap.com/general-sports/set-your-marathon-goals-carefully/#JyEfZ4EuYd2vAlTz.99

http://blog.teamsnap.com/general-sports/set-your-marathon-goals-carefully/

http://www.sciencedaily.com/releases/2013/06/130624075854.htm

http://www.sportscoachingbrain.com/make-it-count/

http://www.sportscoachingbrain.com/make-it-count/Self-confidence

http://www.100breaths.com/How.htm

http://www.theemotionmachine.com/4-mental-exercises-olympic-athletes-use-to-gain-that-extra-edge

http://www.huffingtonpost.com/dr-joann-dahlkoetter/dr-joanns-mental-training_b_3753029.html

http://www.apxstrength.com/#!

http://www.mensfitness.com/kim-tranell/hey-athletes-ever-choke-under-pressure-try-this

http://sportscoachradio.com/wrestlings-dan-gable-olympic-gold-medallist-as-athlete-coach/#sthash.vo3tTGoS.dpufhttp://sportscoachradio.com/wrestlings-dan-gable-olympic-gold-medallist-as-athlete-coach/

http://jeffbeals.wordpress.com/2013/10/04/recovery-is-one-of-the-five-rs-of-your-professional-success/

http://lexfridman.com/blogs/training/tag/dan-gable/http://search.aol.com/aol/search?q=why+admire+dan+gable&s_it=webmail-searchbox&page=2&oreq=0a01f8290cc845f7997ec8126a11268a&v_t=webmail-searchbox

http://www.brainyquote.com/quotes/authors/d/dan_gable.html#45fLi0cEYwoO0FZ4.99

http://sportsmedicine.about.com/cs/sport_psych/a/aa010603a.htm

http://www.perfectbreathing.com/breathing-sports-performance

https://twitter.com/Sports_Greats

http://blogs.psychcentral.com/mindfulness/2012/03/the-mental-workout-100-seconds-to-greater-health-happiness-and-success

http://sirc.ca/newsletters/july12/documents/Free/10%20Minute%20Toughness.pdf

http://www.runnersworld.com/sports-psychology/can-you-talk-yourself-out-of-exhaustion

http://sportsmedicine.about.com/cs/sport_psych/a/aa010603a.htm

http://www.perfectbreathing.com/breathing-sports-performance

http://www.bulletproofmusician.com/how-to-make-performance-anxiety-an-asset-instead-of-a-liability/

http://www.theemotionmachine.com/4-mental-exercises-olympic-athletes-use-to-gain-that-extra-edge

http://www.huffingtonpost.com/dr-joann-dahlkoetter/dr-joanns-mental-training_b_3753029.html

http://www2.canada.com/topics/bodyandhealth/story.html?id=7071787

http://www.bellperformance.com/blog/bid/112134/Passion-Motivation-and-Action-Things-We-Can-All-Use

http://www.youtube.com/watch?v=-WmNHGA5jh8
http://www.youtube.com/watch?v=T9QPMy__xKQ & NR=1
http://www.nba.com/jordan/clareonjordan.html

http://www.goodreads.com/author/quotes/16823.Michael_Jordan?page=2

http://articles.philly.com/2013-12-08/sports/44946908_1_toy-soldiers-fatima-football-games

http://www.jsonline.com/sports/packers/psychologists-ponder-play-of-packers-without-aaron-rodgers-b99157865z1-234924731.html#ixzz2myQSY0aG

http://www.jsonline.com/sports/packers/psychologists-ponder-play-of-packers-without-aaron-rodgers-b99157865z1-234924731.html

http://www.performancemattersinc.com/posts/what-makes-a-champion/

http://www.boxingscene.com/motivation/13780.php

http://www.leadtheteam.net/blog/leadership/the-champion-mindset-the-11-traits/ -- bizz

http://en.wikipedia.org/wiki/List_of_career_achievements_by_Michael_Jordan

http://en.wikipedia.org/wiki/Wilma_Rudolph

http://www.biography.com/people/wilma-rudolph-9466552

http://en.wikipedia.org/wiki/Bruce_Lee

http://www.brainyquote.com/quotes/authors/b/bruce_lee.html

http://topdocumentaryfilms.com/bruce-lee-in-his-own-words/

http://en.wikipedia.org/wiki/Nadia_Com%C4%83neci

http://gymnastics.about.com/od/famousgymnasts/p/nadiacomaneci.htm

http://www.biography.com/people/nadia-comaneci-9254240

http://dangable.com/

http://en.wikipedia.org/wiki/Dan_Gable

http://www.hawkeyesports.com/sports/m-wrestl/mtt/gable_dan00.html

http://www.history.com/this-day-in-history/wrestling-legend-dan-gable-is-
born

http://en.wikipedia.org/wiki/Michael_Jordan

http://www.biography.com/people/michael-jordan-9358066

http://www.washingtonpost.com/wp-srv/sports/nba/longterm/jordan/articles/
jordan14.htm

http://www.nba.com/jordan/clareonjordan.html

http://bilmoore.com/2011/10/25/top-10-traits-of-a-champion/

http://www.wayofchampions.com/articles-by-jerry-lynch/what-makes-a-
champion.html

http://www.eileens-sunsations.com/mi_assets/
Top10QualitiesOfAChampiondebi_moore.pdf

http://www.active.com/triathlon/Articles/How-to-Train-Like-a-Champion

http://www.brainyquote.com/quotes/topics/topic_fitness.
html#LZjZTzJcyrDiu7jT.99 http://www.brainyquote.com/quotes/
topics/topic_fitness3.html#wrMkR4WdxourJ2qw.99

http://www.catalystathletics.com/articles/article.php?articleID=136

http://www.y-e-sports.orgBr J Sports Med 2010;44:i55-i56 doi:10.1136/
bjsm.2010.078725.186 tt. http://bjsm.bmj.com/content/44/Suppl_1/
i55.4.abstract

http://www.y-e-sports.com

https://www.apa.org/helpcenter/sport-psychologists.aspx

http://www.army.mil/article/103420/

http://www.peaksports.com/sports-psychology-case-studies/

http://sportsmedicine.about.com/gi/dynamic/offsite.htm?zi=1/
XJ&sdn=sportsmedicine&zu=http%3A%2F%2Fwww.ultranet.
com%2F%7Edupcak%2Fsprtpsych.html

http://www.athleticinsight.com/Vol1Iss2/Cognitive_Behavioral_Anxiety.htm

http://www.ppoline.co.uk/encyc/sports-psychology.html

http://www.usrowing.org/uploads/docs/15b-1.pdf

http://www.usrowing.org/uploads/docs/15-00b.pdf

http://www.usrowing.org/resourcelibrary/index.aspx

http://healthpsych.psy.vanderbilt.edu/MentalTough.htm

www.americanboardofsportpsychology.org/Portals/24/absp-journalaidman1.
pdf

http://epilepsytalk.com/2012/12/21/epilepsy-triumphs/

http://www.brainyquote.com/quotes/authors/w/wilma_rudolph.
html#t8CphOqtGIICSmSx.99

http://www.interaksyon.com/interaktv/analysis-what-makes-a-champion

https://www.srpl.net/the-undefeated-mindset-of-a-champion/

https://www.youtube.com/watch?v=XkoaJQJb-14

http://www.huffingtonpost.com/steve-siebold/five-olympian-
mindsets_b_4675609.html

http://www.thetimes.co.uk/tto/public/ceo-summit/article3442266.ece

http://www.ansc.purdue.edu/courses/communicationskills/leaderqualities.pdf

http://www.brainyquote.com/quotes/quotes/a/arnoldschw166118.html

http://www.brainyquote.com/quotes/quotes/m/muhammadal148629.html

http://www.brainyquote.com/quotes/authors/n/novak_djokovic.html

http://www.brainyquote.com/quotes/authors/h/harvey_mackay.html

http://quotespictures.com/never-let-the-fear-of-striking-out-get-in-your-way-
babe-ruth-sports-quote/

Mind Over Head Chatter:

A SIX-WEEK COURSE TO ATHLETIC SUCCESS!

Overview

Ever thought that being a successful athlete boiled down to nothing more than talent? Have you found yourself buckling under the pressure of being an athlete and giving in to the self-doubt and anxiety that may be clouding your mind?

That's precisely why you should be glad you're doing this *Mind Over Head Chatter* companion course!

Upon completion of this six-week course, you will be able to:

1. Understand how to ignite your passion so you can go after your goals.

2. Know how to achieve a winning mindset – the kind that can help you become mentally tough when you need it the most.

3. Build the kind of support group that will help you remain confident and motivated, no matter the circumstances.

4. Know how to set the most powerful goals on your journey to athletic success.

5. Create a personal highlight reel of your achievements, accomplishments and wins in life.

6. Emulate the greatest athletes, from their mental toughness to their discipline and determination.

In this six-week course, we will cover the following topics:

- Introduction

- Week One: Building Your Passion

- Week Two: Building Your Social Support

- Week Three: Creating Your Personal Highlight Reel

- Week Four: How To Set Powerful Goals

- Week Five: Building Your Mental Toughness

- Week Six: How to Emulate Great Athletes

- Your Mind Over Head Chatter Worksheet

Introduction

As an athlete, you are often asked to handle significant pressures in your everyday life. Pressure to be bigger. Faster. Stronger. With so much pressure weighing in, it's no wonder so many athletes often lose touch with the passion and fire that inspired them in the first place.

Athletes may seem outwardly confident in their own skills, but as an athlete yourself, you know that there's plenty of room for self-doubt and anxiety in your head. Perhaps you beat yourself up too much after a race, or maybe you were injured during training and now you're having a hard time getting back into the swing of things. No matter the reason, it's completely normal to find yourself plagued by self-doubt, anxiety, and the pressure to succeed.

Luckily, that's where this six-week course comes into play. This course — designed as a companion piece to *Mind Over Head Chatter* by Greg Justice (that's me!) – is designed to help athletes of all ages, skillsets and talent levels to overcome the prevalent fear and anxiety that can prevent them from achieving real success. Throughout the next six weeks, you will learn the following vital tips and techniques:

- How to get back in touch with the passion that inspired you to become an athlete in the first place.

- How to build a powerful support system that will give you the assistance you need to push harder and faster.

- How to create a personal highlight reel of all your past successes, so you never give in to any of the self-doubt that plagues your head.

- How to set goals that are so powerful, you'll not only achieve them – you'll feel like you were forced to achieve them.

- How to build your mental toughness so that you're able to achieve a "winning mindset" – the kind of mindset that makes it possible for you to push forward in your athletic endeavors while silencing any doubt in your head.

- How to emulate your favorite athlete and learn valuable lessons that can be applied to your own life.

Remember, this six-week course is designed to be a companion piece to *Mind Over Head Chatter*. If you're ever confused about any topics brought up during this course, please refer back to the book to help understand these ideas again. All techniques, tips and ideas in this course are based off the information in my book.

Ready to get started? Then let's move right on to Week One!

WEEK ONE: Building Your Passion

When it comes to achieving greatness, many athletes credit their success to two factors:

1. Having the support of someone important in their lives; and/or

2. Having the kind of passion and motivation that keeps driving them forward.

Whether you're just beginning your journey as an athlete or you already have a few ribbons and medals under your belt, it's important to begin this course by connecting with your passions and identifying your support system. These factors are the things that will give you the fuel to keep fighting, even when the going gets tough.

For example, let's say you're working on shaving 30 minutes from your marathon time. Your next race is in two months – that means you're determined to spend the next eight weeks working on getting faster and stronger. You go for longer runs, you start lifting weights, and you eat as clean a diet as possible in order to give yourself the fuel you need to succeed.

However, when the day of the marathon comes around, you only end up shaving roughly 15 minutes from your time.

So what happens next? Do you just give up and accept that you're always going to be stuck at this time? Or do you touch base with your passions, get support and advice from family and loved ones, and keep on with your journey?

By the end of this six-week course, you'll be doing the latter!

Let's start off your first week by identifying one of the best ways to get in touch with the passion and motivation that inspired you to become an athlete in the first place – feeling good about yourself.

It seems like such a simple answer, doesn't it? But it's true; as an athlete, you need to feel inherently good about yourself and the things you do in order to succeed. You need to be your biggest fan. Otherwise, you'll find it all too easy to give into the self-doubt that might still exist in the depths of your mind.

It goes without saying that if you feel good about yourself, you're more likely to propel yourself towards your loftiest goals. There is no crippling self-doubt, there is no negative voice telling you that you can't. Even if those things do creep up every once in awhile, your positive feelings and emotions are more than enough to silence the negative thoughts before they take root.

Now look at the other side of the scale. If you're in a state where you perpetually feel bad about yourself, you're automatically paralyzing every single goal before you've even taken a step towards it.

When you feel bad about yourself, you don't have the strength to stay disciplined when temptation eventually rears its ugly head. For example, say you're training for Nationals. Feeling bad about yourself will prevent you from standing strong against those midnight temptations or training when you're not in a session with your coach.

Let's say that you're a basketball coach. You see the following two kinds of athletes:

- The athletes who will work to the brink of exhaustion. They know that if they push themselves just a bit further, they'll be better rebounders or faster forwards. The hard work, pain and exertion are well worth it, because at the end of the day, they have the kind of self-worth and confidence that gets them through even the most painful practices.

- On the other hand, there are the athletes who need an extra push. Now, as a coach, you might not encounter these athletes too often – especially once you get to the collegiate level. By that time, the majority of athletes still competing typically have a strong sense of inner worth. But occasionally, you might come across a student-athlete who struggles with self-esteem issues. It doesn't just affect the athlete – it affects the entire team.

Which athlete do you want to be? Do you want to be the athlete who goes the extra mile to become better in every way? Do you want to end every practice with sweat pouring out of your body and tears in your eyes from pushing yourself to the limit?

Or do you want to be the athlete who needs to be pushed by a coach to succeed? The one who might cost the entire team the big game, or even the championship?

That's why *Mind Over Head Chatter* is designed to help you turn off the self-doubt and transform your brain into one of the biggest assets you'll use to achieve athletic success!

Let's start by analyzing how to build up your self-confidence so you can get back in touch with your passion and what motivated you in the first place.

When you don't feel good about yourself or believe that you're not worthy of your accomplishments, it sends a signal to the world that you shouldn't be treated with respect and love. It tells the world that you can be taken advantage of because you won't stand up for yourself. It shows everybody that you're not truly ready to unlock your athletic potential.

…Because deep down, you believe you don't deserve to be the best.

But I'm here to tell you otherwise.

It's time to stop letting fear and self-doubt impede your life agenda. It's time to put an end to the tortured doubt and "what-ifs" that circulate your mind every day. You only have this one life to enjoy — there are no timeouts or do-overs. We have one shot to get it right. Isn't that blessing alone enough to make you want to shed the shackles of fear that keep you chained to anything less than your best performance?

Now that I've got you fired up, it's time to identify why you might feel self-doubt and negativity. So what is the number one cause of why you're suffering from this self-doubt rather than enjoying a truly stellar athletic performance?

It's simple: you've disconnected from your life.

When you're truly engaged in your life – that means taking advantage of the numerous blessings, friendships, and opportunities that are presented to you each and every day – there's just no time for negativity; you naturally feel good. That's partially why experts recommend keeping busy after a devastating break-up or loss – our body's natural response to keeping busy is to be positive.

But that kind of engagement is superficial at best. The life engagement I'm talking about here means being 110% involved with your game and appreciating everything that's been thrown your way – be it for better or for worse.

If you're disengaged from your life, it may feel disingenuous or pointless to shift back into gear. Yet with time, effort and a little introspection, you'll find yourself truly connecting with the beautiful world around you and all of its many wonders and blessings. As a result, you'll start to feel good about yourself again.

This can have a trickle-down effect on your athletic performance. When you feel good about who you are as a person, you feel better about who you are as an athlete. There's no separation between the two. Your personal life has a direct impact on your athletic life, and vice versa.

Exercise 1.1

Don't believe that your athletic performance is suffering from inner anxieties and doubts? Think you don't have any *mind chatter* going on in your own head?

Let's see about that. This first week's exercise is going to focus on identifying the mind chatter that might be holding you back from achieving athletic success. Using a pen and a piece of paper or an open Word document, answer the following questions:

- Why did you wake up this morning?

- What's suffering in your life?

- What are your unmet needs and wants?

- What drives you?

- What burdens do you harbor from earlier life stages?

- Do you have a passion for your sport?

Take a closer look at the answers to these questions. You'll start to realize that much of what burdens you or bothers you comes from an inward place. In other words, innate fears, doubts and anxieties you have about yourself.

That's the root cause of your negativity. Like a weed, we're going to pull this negativity up from the ground and plant a seed of growth, passion, and power in its place.

Let's take a closer look at the feelings that are truly keeping you chained to negativity and how you can release yourself and embrace your inner potential and passion:

Lack Of Focus: Think about the last time you truly wanted something. Didn't the sense of focus make you feel energized? Didn't it give you the motivation you needed to surmount the impossible obstacles that were placed in your path?

Even the greatest athletes can suffer from a lack of focus. But if you want to reignite the passion for your game, you have to get focused on your goals again (don't worry, we'll discuss goal-setting in a later week). Focus will help keep you disciplined and determined, no matter what obstacles might be in your way.

Negative Dialogue: Everyone – and I mean *everyone* – suffers from negative self-talk at some point in their lives. You know what I'm talking about here; the kind of inner dialogue that fills you with doubt, fear and anxiety. However, there's a difference between suffering from and rising above an occasional bout of negative dialogue...

…And being so crippled by it that it has paralyzed you from achieving your maximum potential.

Negative self-talk can range from a minor annoyance to downright toxic. I'll show you a few examples so you can see just how damaging a negative internal dialogue can be:

- "I'll never make varsity. I don't know why I even bother trying."

- "Why don't I ever get first place? Any time I think I'm close, someone else wins it. I'll always be in second place."

- "My competitor seems much more accomplished than I am. I might as well give up and save myself the embarrassment."

- "Why should I bother training? I'll never be as good as I want to be."

- "I'll go ahead and let another player on my team take the lead during games. I don't think I'm capable of doing it myself."

See how this negative self-talk can range from mildly pervasive to toxic and harmful?

No matter what kind of negative inner dialogue you're grappling with, it is highly likely that it is crippling your game. If you want to put an end to the negativity and start feeling better about yourself – and unlock your athletic potential – you have to actively and consciously put an end to the damaging internal dialogue.

If you want to eliminate the negative inner dialogue in your head – in other words, get rid of that mind chatter – then you need to replace negative statements with what I like to call "Elite Talk."

These are the powerful and positive statements you use to replace the negative talk that may be clouding your mind. Here are a few examples of positive inner statements you can make every time your mind starts to go negative on you:

- Bring it on!

- Relax, I'm going to master this game.

- Just get the ball to me and I'm going to make good things happen.

- Nothing is going to stand between me and the finish line.

- I hope someone is filming me during this game, because I could be hosting a clinic right now!

- I know my competition wants me to mess up, but they're going to end up extremely disappointed!

This talk is essential for creating the kind of positive internal dialogue that makes the difference between normal people and athletes. You need the mindset of a champion, and that can only happen when you fill your brain with positive, uplifting, and inspiring self-talk.

Manipulate Your Mind With Your Body: At first glance, this might sound like an odd technique to use to block out the mental chatter in your mind. But think about how you act right before a big game or a race. Chances are you're completely focused on the task ahead of you. You're staring at the field and imagining yourself succeeding. You've probably stopped talking to others so you can focus on psyching yourself up. You're jumping up and down, warming up your body. Then, right before the game starts – in the last remaining seconds – you tense up, as your whole body is prepared to fight.

In those last few moments, you don't have time to listen to any negative mental chatter that might take up valuable headspace. All you can focus on is what's in front of you and how you're going to achieve your best performance ever.

That's exactly what you need to do every time you think negative mental chatter is bringing you down. Your body can help trick your mind into believing that you're more powerful and confident simply because your mind takes cues from your body, and vice versa.

Try this experiment for a bit. Let's say you're reading this course on your computer at your desk. Slump over your computer so you're slouching, and frown at your screen. Hold that position for a few minutes. Notice what happens to your emotions during that time?

Now, sit up straight and put a smile on your face. Hold that position for a few minutes and think about how you feel. Chances are you feel like you're in a much better mood than you did when you were slouched over and frowning.

Our bodies can have a profound impact on our mind's ability to reflect positive or negative thoughts. If your body is aligned with positive and confident body language (straight back, assertive stance, relaxed smile, etc.), it won't take long for your brain to follow suit. When you start to experience negative or annoying mental chatter, try shifting your body language so that you're aligned with a more positive and productive stance. It might feel a bit awkward at first, but you'd be surprised how quickly your mental chatter will become silent in the face of your calm and confident pose.

Ready to move forward to Week Two? That's right, you're about to learn why a social support system is one of the most powerful tools an athlete could ever have.

WEEK TWO: Building Your Support System

Now that we've identified the best ways to quell any negative mind chatter that might be holding you back, it's time to identify the social support you'll need to remain successful, even when things start to look like they're getting tough.

This will be the main focus of Week Two, where you'll discover why your social relationships matter to your athletic success. What's more, having a strong support system can help fill your mind with the positive self-talk and confidence you need to drive forward. No matter what you want to achieve, you need good people on your side.

Exercise 2.1

Take a moment to identify the people in your life who offer you the most encouragement and support. It doesn't have to be an immediate family member; perhaps one of your best friends is always at your games cheering you on.

Write down the names of at least three to five people that you can always count on to support you. Once you've listed these names, identify three reasons why you consider these people so supportive. Don't be afraid to get as specific as possible. Maybe your mom always greets you at the finish line with a sports drink, or perhaps your coach was your rock during a particularly hard time in your personal life.

Once you've created this list, keep it handy – these are the people who are going to help you through your athletic journey. These people will be there for you no matter what happens. If you ever feel down about yourself, just remember that you have a strong safety net ready to catch you when you fall and give you a push back in the right direction.

It might seem obvious that having a strong support system will help an athlete build a sense of self-confidence or stick to a rigorous training program. Now, there's research to support the fact that the more people in an athlete's corner, the more likely it is for that athlete to improve his or her success in the game.

According to researcher Tim Rees, a study was conducted to examine how the impact of having a strong social support system helped 200 elite golfers improve their performance. The study found that during anxious and stressful matches, golfers who considered themselves to have strong social support played better than those who did not. The results were certainly apparent – the players lacking social averaged an end-of-round score up to three strokes higher than their counterparts.[1]

---

1   http://sportsmedicine.about.com/od/sportspsychology/qt/Support-Confidence.htm

These findings suggest that athletes should invest a considerable amount of time in building their social support, as this can have significant pay-offs in the game. So how exactly can you do that?

Simple, by using these techniques:

- Ask people to be part of your support group. This might seem obvious, but you'd be surprised at how many family members and friends might not know that you're counting on them for support. Start with the people you identified in the previous exercise. Identify your goals and plans, then share this information with the people on your list. Once you share your goals, ask them to support you in your endeavors. You may need to define what you mean by support; for example, do you mean having them in the stands when you compete? Driving you to practice? Giving you advice after a bad day? The more specific you are early on, the more likely it is that you'll receive the kind of support you need down the line.

- If you don't already have a coach, hire one. A coach is someone who will push you further than you may be able to push yourself. A coach is the one person who is 100% invested in your success, as his or her own success is reflected in your performance. If you need someone who is always going to be there for you – rain or shine – and understands the intricacies of your sport, then prioritize finding a qualified coach with a track record of success.

- If you are not able to afford a coach, or you already have one, opt to use a training partner. This person could be someone you've trained with before, or a competitor you're friendly with off the field. Having a training partner can take your game to the next level, since you'll likely compete with him or her during practice. A training partner can push you past your boundaries, which is what you need to improve your athletic performance. What's more, a training partner can help you overcome any mind chatter that might be filling you with self-doubt.

When looking for a training partner, make sure you find someone who competes at a similar level to you. If you really want to challenge yourself, find someone who's slightly better than you. This can give you the push you need during practice to improve your performance, as you'll want to keep up with their level.

- You may also want to consider joining a local sports club or organization to meet like-minded people and athletes. This is a great suggestion for someone who may not be competing at the collegiate or professional level, and may need to find new training partners. Socializing with a group who shares a passion for your sport can help broaden your support network, as you could potentially meet training partners, coaches, and people who are happy to cheer you on in the stands.

If you're having trouble building up your support network, you may need to analyze how your behaviors might be driving people away. Should you be the first one to complain during practice or you're always saying something negative about your performance, people might not want to be in your support network simply because they don't want to deal with your negative attitude. This is why it's so important to eliminate negative mind chatter from your brain, as it has likely found its way out of your mouth. If you want to build a strong social support system, you need to be the kind of athlete that people want to support. That means being positive, gracious, and willing to move on, even after a bad game or match.

Finally, be willing to return the favor. You have to support others in order to build up your own support system. Talk to other athletes you know and see if you can form a "support" group of sorts. Volunteer to go to each other's games to cheer them on. When you take turns cheering on another athlete in the stands, you're much more likely to find more people cheering you on at your own games.

Now that you've identified the beginnings of your social support network and eliminated some of the negative mind chatter in your head, it's time to move forward with the third week.

These lessons are going to set the foundation for your success. Therefore, be sure to incorporate them into your daily life as much as possible. You'll find that as you grow and improve your athletic performance, your mind chatter will be replaced by positive reinforcement and a strong social support system.

WEEK THREE: Creating Your Personal Highlight Reel

Now that you've focused on building your support system – which plays a crucial role in helping you become a more successful athletic – it's time to create your very own personal highlight reel. Think of this as an internal movie that you'll show yourself every time an iota of doubt or nervousness starts to creep into your mind. Your personal highlight reel will be used to remind you of your many successes, and also of your ability to succeed even when that gold medal or blue ribbon seems just out of reach.

Believe me when I say that everyone's capable of making a personal highlight reel, even if you've just started out in your sport of choice. I don't care how many trophies you've won or whether you just started training an hour ago. As a human being, you have shown dogged determination in the face of *something*. It doesn't have to be related to sports – heck, it doesn't even have to be related to anything athletic at all.

If you've done something to defy the odds…if you've achieved a goal that once seemed far too out of reach…if you've ever done something when other people have told you that you couldn't do it…

Then you have plenty of material for your personal highlight reel. This week, we're going to focus on building that personal highlight reel, so you will be able to remind yourself that you're so much stronger than any obstacles or challenges that may be in your way.

You've already achieved wonderful things in your life - things that deserve to be celebrated right here, right now.

How do I know you've done great things? Because I know that right now, you can write down three times in your life that you achieved or overcame something that you thought yourself incapable of.

They don't have to be lofty achievements or movie-worthy accomplishments. In fact, your proudest achievements may have little to do with winning weight-lifting competitions or helping your basketball team earn a conference title. Rather, your greatest achievements could be smaller choices that placed you on the path towards the life that you're leading today.

Exercise 3.1

You've probably guessed what happens next: It's time to create your own list of the accomplishments, small steps, and life choices that have helped you become the athlete you are today (and the athlete you'll become tomorrow!).

Grab a pen and paper – or open a Word document – and start building your list of your previous accomplishments. They don't have to be significant or come in the form of blue ribbons, gold medals, or conference titles. To help you get started, here's an example of great achievements that someone has made to become a more successful and disciplined athlete:

1. "When I rose above the taunting of my bullies. To them, I appeared weak and vulnerable – but to myself, I knew that I was capable of being so much more than what they said."

2. "When I first decided to try out for my high school football team, despite all the teasing I endured as a child. They told me I couldn't do it – but as soon as I showed up on that football field, I proved them wrong."

3. "When I applied for college. As a first-generation student from a bad part of the city, going to college was pretty much considered a luxury. But I knew I wanted better things for myself – and I didn't stop pushing myself even after I had that acceptance letter in my hands."

See how your greatest achievements could vary? It isn't always about earning an award. Instead, it's about doing something that helps you rise above the challenges and obstacles in your life. It's about keeping your journey moving forward rather than giving up. No matter what that means to you, it's an accomplishment that should be celebrated – and it's going to form the basis of your highlight reel.

Now it's time to create your own personal highlight reel. Get started by filling in three achievements that you're proud of:

1. _____

2. _____

3. _____

Once you've prepared your list, carry it with you every day or post it where you can see it throughout your day-to-day routine. The more you look at this list, the easier it will be to create that personal highlight reel that you can turn to whenever you need a little extra motivation.

Your personal highlight reel should help you build momentum towards your goals and silence any negative thoughts. Like a court case, it serves as evidence that you are capable of achieving anything – even if it seems impossible.

Before we move on to Week Three – where you'll learn how to set powerful and effective goals – let's take a moment to talk about something that every athlete needs in order to be successful. You could be as talented as Tiger Woods or Serena Williams, but if you don't have this one skill, you're eventually going to hit a roadblock and get stuck while other athletes keep passing you by.

What's this skill, you ask? Simple – it's **discipline.**

I know it's not the sexiest word in the dictionary, especially when it comes to improving the quality of your physical and mental fitness along with your athletic performance.

But that's just providing you with a map for where you want to go. Think of discipline as the fuel that provides your powerful new mindset with the energy it needs to move forward. Without discipline, it's easy to get lost on the road towards your ultimate success. As you'll learn about in Week Five of this course, my "facts of life" state, discipline will always be the key factor that determines your destiny.

So what exactly does discipline mean? It can be many things:

- For the athlete, discipline means having the strength to push themselves past their limit. It means never settling for what's comfortable – our bodies only change when we push ourselves past our peak.

- For the single mother, discipline means having the courage and willpower to actively raise her children, even if she has to work multiple jobs to support them.

- For the freelancer, discipline means sticking to a specific working schedule, no matter how tempting it may be to skip work and go to the beach.

- For the weight-loss pursuer, discipline means sticking to the diet and making a commitment to exercise for at least thirty minutes each day, no matter how tempting it may be to take a day off.

While these four different people may have separate life goals, they all have one thing in common – they understand that discipline is the determining factor in how successful they'll be at reaching their goals.

Discipline means always expecting the best from yourself. Additionally, when you don't perform at your absolute best, discipline always helps you pick yourself right back up from the ground and get back on track, no matter how much of a stumble you may have taken.

For example, if you're trying to shave twenty seconds off of your mile time but you never push yourself to run faster during practices, discipline allows you to learn from your mistakes, make adjustments, and build on things a little more each day until you achieve your ultimate goal.

Again, discipline isn't the most exciting concept in the so-called self-help genre – but it is undeniably the most powerful.

When you expect more from yourself, you perform better. And when you perform better, you move towards your ultimate goals, no matter what they may be. If success had to be displayed as a formula, it would look a little something like this:

Success = Discipline + A Winning Mindset

As you can see, improving your performance or becoming a successful athlete isn't just about being born with natural talent.

It's not about considering yourself especially lucky or blessed by a higher power.

It has nothing to do with your background, the amount of money you have, or the university you attended.

Instead, it has everything to do with your ability to *choose* to take action towards your goals each and every day, no matter how small those actions might be. That is what is at the heart of discipline – your willingness to choose to better yourself with each passing day.

Best of all, your personal highlight reel is always going to be there for you. It's instantly available in your head – all you have to do is mentally press play to remind yourself of all the amazing successes you've already had in your life.

No matter what is bringing you down, your personal highlight reel is there to pick you back up. As you become more and more successful and continue to improve your athletic performance, you can add even more scenes to your personal highlight reel. Soon, you'll have so many successes stored away that you'll hardly even need it, and you will feel confident enough to take on the world!

Now that you've built your personal highlight reel, it's time to move on to Week Four. Over the course of the next week, you'll learn how to set powerful goals and motivate yourself to surpass these goals during each and every practice. The more goals you set and achieve, the more likely it is that cheers will replace any self-doubt and negative mind chatter!

WEEK FOUR: How To Set Powerful Goals

No athlete becomes successful just out of sheer luck; that path is usually forged by determination and hard work. That's what you're about to learn in Week Four – how to set powerful goals that can help you slowly but surely improve your athletic performance.

Before we begin, it's important to remember that not all goals are created equal. There's a difference between a goal that you try to work toward, and a goal that's so well-planned and executed that it's almost effortless to achieve.

To begin Week Four, let's start by setting the goals that will guide your work throughout the week.

Exercise 4.1

For many athletes, learning how to set goals isn't going to be much of a challenge. Perhaps you already have a vague idea of what you'd like to accomplish, like improving your overall time or earning a medal at your next race.

But if you really want to set the most powerful goals possible, it's not enough to have a *vague* idea of your goals – you need to know exactly what you want and how you are going to achieve it.

With that in mind, write down the goals you want to accomplish. Separate those goals according to when you would like to accomplish them (i.e. one month, six months, one year, two years, etc.). List the goals according to when you'd like to achieve them.

When you're writing down your goals, try to be as specific as possible. Don't just write down that you want to improve your mile-time. Instead, figure out how much time you would like to shave from your time every month until the end of the year.

It's okay if you're not exactly sure what to write down at the moment. The point here is to put your goals on paper (or a Word document) so that they exist. Throughout the coming week, we'll work on tweaking your goals until they're ready for you.

———————

Goals, by their nature, are meant to stretch your capabilities. The challenge for you is to understand the balance between a goal that gets you to the next level and the reality of how far you can go today. It is easy to have goals that will definitely stretch you, but in reality end up being so ambitious that you have to abandon them. It is just as easy to set them so low that you have nothing to aspire for and experience no real growth. Selecting your goals is a key component to your overall success as an athlete.

So what do you look at when you have decided that the time has come to prioritize those goals? What are the things you need to consider when it is time to prioritize?

In many cases, it is more appropriate to look at the timing of a goal rather than the importance of the goal. After all, it wouldn't be a goal at all if you didn't want to achieve it eventually!

Selecting and prioritizing your goals should come from the list that you put together in the above exercise. However, throughout the process, you will continue asking yourself these same questions about what your goals are, and as a result, items can be added, subtracted, or reprioritized over time.

My point here is that the process of selecting and prioritizing goals is repetitive. Goals will change as your life changes. You could end up having a child, or simply discover that your goal was actually too easy to achieve. Many things will influence your goal-setting efforts, so don't become so rigid about your goals that they completely crumble in the face of change. Consider prioritization a fluid process with constant ebbs and flows.

If you want to ensure your goal's success, it's important to make sure that you've set goals that are meaningful and appropriate for your life.

Goals need to have personal relevance in your life, even if they are strictly athletic. After all, gold medals and faster times have emotional significance attached to them. For example, a gold medal could mean more opportunities for you and your family. A faster time could be an achievement that celebrates your parents' dedication to providing you with the best life possible.

As you can see, if a goal has a significant emotion or personal recognition attached to it, it's more likely that you'll achieve it than a goal that has no real impact on your life.

After the goals have been set and you begin to implement them, you can take some steps to help ensure success for each.

1) Create a detailed task list of what you need to accomplish

Each goal has a set of sub-goals and objectives. When you look at each of your goals, you have to break them down into smaller, manageable tasks. The best way to do this is to look at what steps logically need to be completed, in what order they need to be completed in.

2) Measure and track

It is very important that you have a mechanism for measuring and tracking your goals as you work through them. Measurement can mean many things. It can refer to the time it takes to get something done or the amount something changes. Regardless of what the measurement is, you need to determine it before you start executing on the goal and then keep track of it throughout.

3) Use the support as needed

If you want to be successful, you can't always do it alone. Understanding your strengths and weaknesses is important. When you need help, you can look to others for support. Family members and friends can provide a great background for support, especially if you're putting in long hours in training and need the emotional and mental benefits that come from healthy interpersonal relationships.

4) Embrace challenges and roadblocks

Things never quite go as planned, no matter how talented you are. Remember this as you start down the path of setting and implementing a goal strategy. When those challenges come, you need to be resilient. Do not let them derail you. Come up with a plan to take out any challenge that may come your way.

5) Reevaluate as needed

A roadmap sometimes needs to be changed. What used to be a straight path may suddenly have a curve. If you don't follow the new path, you could very well lose your way. Don't be afraid to reevaluate your goals if circumstances change or if you decide that you need to reprioritize what you want to accomplish. It is okay to reevaluate and change your goals as needed.

6) Stay on track and remain focused

Staying on track is really important. It is so easy to let the day-to-day tasks of any job get in your way and keep you from focusing on the goals you have set. Make it a daily task to review your goals and what you should have accomplished against those goals. Keep yourself motivated for what you need to accomplish.

7) Reset in order to continue stretching yourself

Remember, you can always set goals and then reset them once you reach them. Assuring that you have aspirational goals that move as your performance improves is very important. You do not want to stay stagnant, so make sure you stretch yourself each time you achieve a goal. Set the next one just a bit higher and keep stretching yourself.

There are going to be times when it seems hard to achieve your goals. Perhaps you've been trying to reach it for so long that you've lost motivation, or maybe you don't think you'll ever achieve it. Whatever the case may be, the tips and techniques contained in this week's lesson will start putting your goal-setting abilities into overdrive.

Fasten your seatbelts, because you're about to leave the goal-achieving fast lane…

And learn how to start building your mental toughness!

WEEK FIVE: Building Your Mental Toughness

We all hear about what a "winning mindset" should look like. People with "winning mindsets" are more likely to be actively involved in the things that matter most to them. They're more likely to be happy. Healthy. Successful. And on their way to the top!

But when it gets down to it, what exactly is a winning mindset? Is it a one-size-fits-all concept, where you have to "fake it until you make it?"

Or should a winning mindset require a separate kind of approach, where each of us has our own certain attitude that propels us closer to the successes that make your athletic accomplishments that much more meaningful?

In Week Five, we're about to learn what it takes to build mental toughness – or as I like to call it, a "winning mindset." Mental toughness isn't about blocking out the world entirely; instead, it's about creating the kind of mindset that minimizes negative chatter and enhances positivity in your life. It's the kind of mindset that knows no matter how many times you fall down, you're always capable of picking yourself back up. In short, it's the mindset of a winning athlete – and that's what you'll focus on building here in Week Five.

You may disagree with me here, but I'm willing to stick my neck out and say it's a bit of both. Winning in and of itself is a finite concept with infinite connotations. In other words, winning can mean earning a blue ribbon at a horse show, placing first in the 400 meter dash or even just getting up in the morning when your body is screaming for you to stay in bed and pull the covers over your head.

However, winning always means pushing yourself to be your very best. So in that case, a winning mindset blends together the traditional definition of "winning" (being your best) with your own personal spin on things (being your best at the things that matter most to you). For example, a winning mindset for an Olympic athlete means having the attitude that allows her to train for hours each day and eat a nutritional diet. On the other hand, a winning mindset for a cancer patient means having the strength to live his life each day and continue doing the things he loves without letting the illness take over his life.

In that respect, there is no such thing as a one-size-fits-all winning mindset. The sooner you embrace this realization, the sooner you can find the winning mindset that will unlock your true potential.

I've found that people who have optimized their winning mindset are often those who believe in the Bigger Picture. Without the Bigger Picture, we're more susceptible to the daily influences and judgments that try to label us and stuff us in a limiting box. When we define ourselves by how many medals we've earned or how we stack up to someone else, we begin to lose sight of the truly wonderful potential each and every one of us has within themselves. We realize that personal dramas don't matter. We accept that we are capable of making mistakes – and when we do, it's not the end of the world.

On that note, I want to point out what should always be the first step towards achieving your own winning mindset – accepting the fact that you *will* make bad decisions, mistakes and missteps. In that light, it becomes obvious that we should expect to earn a few bumps and bruises on the path we call life – and if we do, we don't have to punish ourselves for it. Instead, we can pick ourselves up, dust ourselves off and get right back on track with the knowledge that while we may not be perfect, we're perfectly capable of moving on from our past mistakes.

To achieve a winning mindset, it's important to let go of your past, no matter how much you think it played a role in forming the person you are today. Don't put a good or bad label on any of your past behaviors or experiences. Instead, simply derive meaning from it.

For example, if you lost a big race or came from a background where you didn't have access to the best training possible, don't let these experiences teach you to abuse or fear the love of others. Derive meaning from the experience. Show yourself how much of a stronger person you are because of the experience. Write down the life lessons you've learned that have helped you become a better person. Even if you don't believe in the lessons you're writing down, do it anyway. Sometimes it takes seeing it on paper to realize just how much we can be influenced by our past, and how past experiences can keep us emotionally and mentally paralyzed.

Adopting a winning mindset also involves accepting the things in life that are out beyond your control. I like to call these things "the facts of life" – and more often than not, they deal with toxic scenarios and situations that are designed to drag you down from being the best you can be. For example, if you find that you're constantly comparing yourself to other athletes, you haven't yet accepted the "facts of life," there will always be toxic dramas designed to distract you from achieving your best life. There will always be someone who is bigger or faster than you. Accepting the "facts of life" means that you're relinquishing control over the things that you really have no control over.

As soon as you do that, you'll be able to focus on creating your winning mindset and applying it to every facet of your life from training and diet to personal health and fitness.

Here's a snapshot of just a few of these "facts of life." Read them over and over until you've memorized them – the sooner you can accept the "facts of life," the sooner you can let go of the doubt and lack of confidence that is keeping you from being your absolute best:

1. Don't blame others for your feelings, emotions, experiences and problems.

2. Don't expect others to rescue you, or give you what you want. Work to earn your own way.

3. You are not entitled to anything.

4. You mind, body and spirit don't simply deteriorate with age. Lack of exercise in any of these areas causes deterioration.

5. Don't give adults a pacifier because of perceived bad experiences. Instead, give them a push.

6. No one completes you. You are not incomplete.

7. You have to make the decision as to whether you choose to be a contender or a pretender.

8. Discipline will always be a key factor that determines your destiny.

9. If you don't take near-constant action, you are asking for disaster.

10. Every day, you either get a little better or a little worse.

11. You really do seal your fate by the choices you make.

12. The best way to stand out is to be different from the crowd.

In many instances, we doubt our ability to believe in our power and strength to move to the next level. But engaging in your winning mindset means believing in your own strength to win, no matter how lofty the goal or obstacle in front of you might be.

Now that we've explored how to build mental toughness and adopt a winning mindset, let's move on to the last week of the *Mind Over Head Chatter* course. In the next week, you'll discover how to emulate the greatest athletes in the world in terms of their discipline, dedication, and ability to rise above any obstacles in their way.

WEEK SIX: How to Emulate Great Athletes

Congratulations – Week Six is finally here! If you've made it this far, you've learned some pretty tough lessons and exercises, all of which have been dedicated to helping you become the A+ athlete you were always meant to be. You've built on important lessons about how to minimize negative head chatter, improve your performance during practice, set powerful goals, and build a strong social support system.

So what can you expect for this week?

It's a fun one, in my opinion. In Week Six, we're going to talk about the importance of emulating great athletes, no matter what sport they play. Notice for a moment that I said *emulate*, not worship. There's a big difference between hero worship – where your role model can do no wrong, even when he or she has displayed awful behaviors – and emulation, where you use your athlete as a platform for learning important lessons and behaviors that can be applied in your own life.

There's another distinct difference between hero worship and emulation. With the former, you're likely to view the athlete's accomplishments as your own. In other words, if he or she wins a match, you'll feel like you won as well. Suddenly, you're holding that athlete's performance as more important than your own – and that can have a significant impact on your game.

Emulation, on the other hand, teaches you to derive important meaning from your favorite athlete's experiences so you can apply it to your own life. If your favorite athlete gets embroiled in a personal scandal, you'll learn that it's always important to be a good person, whether you're on or off the field. Should your athletic hero's performance suddenly take a dive, you can use this as a lesson about the importance of continued improvement (or at the very least, how to retire gracefully).

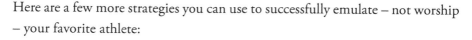

Exercise 6.1

Before we dive into strategies, let's take a minute to focus on who your favorite athletes are and why. Grab a piece of paper and a pen – or just open your trusty Word document – and begin writing down the names of athletes who you genuinely admire.

Don't just settle for the athletes who happen to be popular at the moment. If you've never stopped loving Michael Jordan, go ahead and add him to the list. If you admire a local athlete, add him or her to the list as well.

Once you've created your list of athletes you respect, write down at least three reasons why you admire them. Get specific about these reasons, as these people have to justify why they're on your list.

As a quick rule of thumb, if you can't come up with three genuine reasons why someone should be on your list, eliminate them altogether.

Once you have your list, move on to the rest of Week Six.

Here are a few more strategies you can use to successfully emulate – not worship – your favorite athlete:

- Use the athlete to set the bar high in your own life. Instead of seeing your favorite athlete as someone who is completely untouchable – and therefore, intimidating – see him or her as an example to follow. Study up on the athlete's diet, discipline, and practice regimen. While you don't have to copy them exactly (especially if they're professional and you're just starting out in the sport), they can give you a good idea of the hard work and dedication it takes to get to that level.

- Look for other athletes who are similar to your role model. Ideally, you want to find as many athletes as possible to emulate, as there are different lessons you can learn from each individual. You don't have to find athletes who encompass every lesson you'd like to learn; instead, find athletes who display characteristics you'd like to emulate in your own life. For example, maybe there's one athlete whose dedication you admire, while another may have a great sense of team spirit. There's no rule that says you have to stick to just one role model, so feel free to expand your horizons.

- Think about what it is about that athlete that resonates with you. When you first heard of that athlete, what immediately stuck out to you? What did you admire the most? Getting in touch with the reasons why that athlete speaks to you can help you identify the qualities and characteristics you'd like to display in your own life.

- Don't limit your search for a role model to the professional or even collegiate level – an ideal athlete can be someone who trains in your gym, or even your coach or personal trainer. There's inspiration everywhere, so don't limit yourself to just one type of athlete.

- If you get the chance to connect with the athlete you want to emulate, don't be afraid to ask for advice or guidance about how you can improve your own performance. Athletes are often more than happy to help others with their own performance, so don't feel as if you're crossing a line. Of course, you should be mentally prepared to be let down by your role model. For example, if you get the chance to approach a professional athlete and they brush you off, don't take it personally. They're human beings after all, and they might not have the time or the energy to give everyone the personal attention that they want.

Remember, there are important lessons to be learned when you emulate your athletic role model. Study how that athlete approaches various challenges in his or her life, and seek to embrace those types of behaviors in your own life. Tweak his or her behaviors to match your own life and personality type. After all, you're not seeking to become an identical clone of your favorite athlete; you're simply trying to learn important lessons from his or her life and see what works for you.

As you can see, Week Six is a fun and simple week dedicated to helping you put those finishing touches on all the important lessons you've learned throughout the past six weeks. It's meant to help you finally put what you've learned into action – and now that you've reached the end of the *Mind Over Head Chatter* course, you're ready to start building your support network...

Set more powerful goals...

Achieve peak performance levels...

And unlock the kind of benefits that are only possible when your mind truly believes in your ability to become a success.

So now that you've finished the *Mind Over Head Chatter* six-week course, there's only one question I have for you:

Are you ready to bring your A-game?

Your Mind Over Head Chatter Worksheet

Now that you've completed this special six-week supplement course to my book, *Mind Over Head Chatter*, it's time to start putting what you've learned to good use with this special worksheet.

In the following worksheet, write down your goals, along with a timeline of when you want to achieve these goals. This worksheet will help you keep track of your goals over the coming weeks, as well as provide you the opportunity to make any changes to them so you can continue to push yourself.

Mind Over Head Chatter Worksheet

DATE: _____

MY GOALS:

1. _____
2. _____
3. _____
4. _____
5. _____

* * * * *

OF THE GOALS I JUST IDENTIFIED, MY MOST IMPORTANT ONE IS:

_____

I AM GIVING MYSELF _____ MONTHS TO ACHIEVE THIS GOAL.

I PLAN ON MAKING THE FOLLOWING CHANGES TO ACHIEVE THIS GOAL

_____

_____

I WILL USE THE FOLLOWING TRAINING PLAN:

_____

_____

I AM FOLLOWING THIS TRAINING PLAN BECAUSE:

_____

_____

I WILL DESIGNATE_____AS MY WEEKLY DAY TO TRACK MY GOAL'S PROGRESS

ABOUT THE AUTHORS

Greg Justice is a best-selling author, speaker, and fitness entrepreneur and was inducted into the National Fitness Hall of Fame in 2017. He opened AYC Health & Fitness, Kansas City's original personal training center, in May 1986.

Greg is the co-founder and CEO of the **National Corporate Fitness Institute** (NCFI), a certifying body for fitness professionals, and the co-founder of **Scriptor Publishing Group**.

He has been actively involved in the fitness industry since the early 1980's as a club manager, owner, personal fitness trainer, and sports conditioning specialist at the collegiate and professional level.

Greg writes articles for many publications and websites, is a featured columnist for *Corporate Wellness* magazine, and *Personal Fitness Professional* magazine. He is the author of several books including *Mind Over Fatter: The Psychology of Weight Loss, Mind Your Own Fitness: A Mindful Approach To Exercise, Lies & Myths About Corporate Wellness,* and *Treadside Manner: Confessions Of A Serial Personal Trainer.*

Greg holds a master's degree in HPER (exercise science) and a bachelor's degree in Health & Physical Education from Morehead State University, Morehead, KY.

Greg is available for speaking engagements on a variety of health and fitness topics. You may contact Greg at info@gregjustice.com or visit www.GregJustice.com for more information.

Art Still is a writer, speaker and CEO of Still 4 Life, an ecommerce business that believes in "paying it forward".

He was born and raised in Camden, New Jersey where he graduated from Camden High School in 1974.

Art was a four year starter at the University of Kentucky, where he was named SEC Player of the Year and Consensus All-American as a senior. He was inducted into the College Football Hall of Fame in 2015.

In 1978, Art was the first round draft pick of the Kansas City Chiefs and played 12 seasons in the NFL with the Chiefs and Buffalo Bills. He was selected to four Pro-Bowls, was a two time MVP, and inducted into the Kansas City Chiefs Hall of Fame in 1997.

In addition to a very active family life, Art has taken on various projects since he left the game, including charity work with several organizations. Still remains connected with football serving as one of the Kansas City Chiefs ambassadors. In that role he is frequently out and about in the community with other former players. "You get an opportunity to work in the community with a variety of charities and groups of people," said Still, who has been married to wife Liz since 1983. "We enjoy doing things that are positive and something that will be lasting in helping others. We do a lot of benefits and working with youths and their families."